MW00677298

Other publications and assessments by
Patrick Handley, Ph.D.

—

Book:

INSIGHT
…into your personality strengths

—

Self-scoring assessment and interpretative booklets:
INSIGHT Inventory
(paper self-scoring strengths-based personality assessment)

—

Online assessments and reports
INSIGHT Inventory–SELF Report
(online strengths-based personality assessment)

INSIGHT Inventory–OBSERVER Feedback Report
(online assessment for observer rating of user)

INSIGHT Inventory–TEAM Profile Map
(online assessment for observer rating of user)

—

Increasing Team Engagement
Insight Team Development Modules
(Set of 12 self-guided, structured team engagement activities)

LEAD

with

INSIGHT

...and become the leader you want to be

Complete the INSIGHT Inventory and gain
insight into your personality strengths,
learn how others see you, and
eliminate behaviors that block
your success.

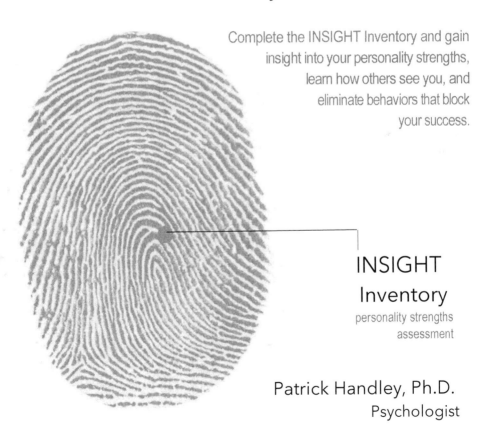

INSIGHT
Inventory
personality strengths
assessment

Patrick Handley, Ph.D.
Psychologist

The names and identifying details of individuals sited in examples of this book have been changed to maintain confidentiality.

Insight Institute Press
A division of Insight Institute, Inc.
7205 N.W. Waukomis Drive
Kansas City, MO 64151

For information about special discounts for bulk purchases, please contact Insight Institute, Inc., at 1.800.861.4769

Manufactured in the United States of America

1   3   5   7   9   10   8   6   4   2

Library of Congress Cataloging-in-Publication Data
Handley, Patrick

LEAD with INSIGHT
and become the leader you want to be

1. Leadership—business—management
2. Self—actualization

ISBN-978-0-9961246-2-1

Dedication

To my family; wife Melanie, daughter Lauren, and son Shea who supported my efforts, cheered me forward, all the while providing many personal and humorous examples of personality strengths and triggers in action.

To my doctoral advisors at the University of Missouri, Dr. Joseph Johnston and Dr. Norm Gysbers who were all pioneers in positive psychology long before the movement was popularized. And, to Dr. Tom Krieshock at the University of Kansas who helped manage the statistical analysis and offered guidance on career and self-discovery throughout the development of the INSIGHT Inventory.

To Austin Schauer who helped compile my writings, speeches, and manuals that spanned over three decades of work and pulled these together in one place shaping the original draft. His family stories provided some of the more unbelievable case examples; he assures me they are true. And, to Starla Lewis who has spent over fifteen years working with the Insight Institute, Inc.

A special thanks to all the "leaders in the making" who attended my seminars over the past thirty-five years and shared their stories about personality traits, strengths, and differences. Thank you for investing your time and attention in learning how to Lead with Insight.

And, to you the reader for your interest and selection of this book. You make it all possible.

The three of you go down the road,
as down the road go you,
the one you know,
the one they see,
and the one you want to be.

John Masefield, 1890

The three of you will journey to "insight" through the three parts of this book.

PART 1: "the one you know"

> *insight into how you see yourself; your identity*

PART 2: "the one they see"

> *insight into how others view you; your reputation*

PART 3: "the one you want to be"

> *insight into how to unleash the unique you; your destiny*

LEAD with INSIGHT

Prefix

Exceptional leaders have insight into their personality strengths, insight into how others see them, and insight into strategies for eliminating the hot buttons, triggers, and anger outbursts that may derail their success. When these leaders make mistakes they learn from them and get back on track quickly. Plus, these leaders develop methods for bringing out the best in others. They lead with insight.

The word "insight" is defined by the Oxford English Dictionary as "the capacity to have a deep intuitive understanding." Preeminent psychologist Gordon Allport defined insight as "the ability to look inside and see yourself as others see you."

This book and the accompanying *INSIGHT Inventory-SELF* assessment and *INSIGHT Observer Feedback* charts will help you clarify how you see your personality strengths and use them in leadership tasks. The *INSIGHT Observer Feedback* charts and discover how you come across to others. The comparison of these two perspectives reveals key information needed to develop true insight.

For many leaders, the biggest obstacle in developing deeper insight may be the mistaken belief that they already have it. In his landmark book, *Good to Great*, Tom Collins opens the first chapter by noting that "good is the enemy of great." He emphasizes that when leaders believe they are doing well, they frequently stop practicing the very behaviors that helped them achieve success and that are needed to help them become great. You need to avoid that misstep also. Whatever your current level of insight is, you can get better, you can increase your understanding yourself and others. You can use these new levels of insight to positively transform your work relationships.

Insight includes the ability to not only see your strengths, but also to stay in your strengths zone. If you get there, but you cannot stay there, you'll wander off your path to success. You will stumble into hot buttons, triggers, and anger outbursts and get lost in derailing and self-sabotaging behaviors. Finding your way back can be a bumpy road. True insight into your strengths involves not only getting there, but staying there.

When you practice mindfulness, you see day-to-day thoughts, feelings, and behaviors from an elevated perspective. The meaning in the smallest of interactions will become clear to you. You will experience a shift from "reacting" to "responding." As you develop deeper insight into your strengths, you will be ever mindful of ways to stay in that special zone where you perform and communicate at your best.

When you increase your insight into your personality strengths, you become the leader your organization and team needs. You develop the skill to consciously transform relationships with co-workers, team members, and other managers. You become the leader you want to be. You LEAD with INSIGHT.

LEAD with INSIGHT

... and become the leader you want to be

Table of Contents

LEAD with INSIGHT

LEAD with INSIGHT

The three of you go down the road,
As down the road go you,
the one you know,
the one they see,
and the one you want to be.

modification of poem by
John Masefield, 1890

—/ /—

Introduction

As this ageless poem declares, we are all journeying down the road of
life striving to become "the one we want to be," the leader we
envision being, and the team member we hope to be, the work
associate that communicates well with others. The three key phrases
of the poem serve as the headings for the three parts of this book.
Perhaps the words will call you to reflect upon your current journey
of self-discovery and identify ways to speed along more successfully.

There are indeed three of you going down the road of life. The first is, "the one you know." This is your self-concept and identity. It's the person you see in the mirror. The second person going down the road with you is "the one they see." Others view you through their own unique perspectives and colored lenses. The one they see is your social identity or reputation. You need to know who the person is that others see. Then there is the third person, the most important sojourner; the "one you want to be." Fully becoming that person will help you unleash the "unique," true you.

This book guides you in discovering more about all three persons going down the road. It helps you move more effectively and positively, perhaps with a bounce in your step, down the path of life. Uncovering and becoming your best self will help you be a stronger leader, a more positive team member, and a more productive co-worker. Outside of work you'll also become a better spouse, a more loving parent, and a more engaged friend. Unleashing your unique personality strengths contributes to improved relationships in all aspects of life. This helps create a better world for all of us. It's well worth the effort.

To get you started down the road, an access code to the *INSIGHT Inventory* self-rating will help you discover more about yourself. Included in Part 2 are several *Insight Observer Feedback* charts for requesting feedback from others. These will guide you through an in-depth exploration of how you are seen by others.

Part One helps you assess your view of "the one you know" and clarify your strengths. This is important because it's difficult to unleash your uniqueness until you have clearly identified your personality strengths. You must know yourself and live your strengths.

Part Two helps you better understand how others see you. Your reputation with others defines much of who you are. The Chapters guide you in exploring the differences between the perceptions other people have of you and how you see yourself. You'll integrate these two perspectives in ways that build upon your strengths. You may even discover that others can see some of your strengths better than you see them yourself.

Part Three provides a roadmap for becoming the person you want to be. You'll examine how you get derailed and triggered into using ineffective behaviors. When your hot buttons get pushed, you'll tend to move out of your strengths zone and head in the wrong direction. This book will help you return to your strongest self and develop a strategy to stay there, in your strengths zone.

Why I wrote this book

Most of my 35-year career as a psychologist has been spent working in the area of positive psychology and personality strengths assessment. My primary focus has been helping organizations develop more effective leaders, increase team performance, and grow talent at all employee levels. This involves helping people identify their strengths and teaching them how to stay in the zone where they can perform at their best.

This book will help you more fully discover your true personality strengths. When this happens, you will build upon your work success, enhance your relationships, and increase your own inner happiness. Lean forward, stay open, and you'll discover new pathways to unleashing the best in yourself and others.

There are four key steps.
Get:
  1) Strong—discover your personality strengths.
  2) Accurate—learn how others see you.
  3) Free—eliminate behaviors that block your success.
  4) Skilled—identify ways to communicate better.

All of us as humans are full of unlimited potential. Hopefully this book will help you become more fascinated with yourself, thrilled about discovering your "true you" and excited about charging ahead in your life-long journey of becoming who you want to be.

It has been said that a life lived true to yourself with a continuous unfolding of strengths is the most fulfilling and successful. I hope this book will help you walk a bit faster in getting to where you want to be and fully discover all the many shades and colors in your personality fingerprint.

I wrote this book reveals your unique strengths as a leader. When this happens, good things unfold at work and in your personal life. Plus, there is a powerful secondary benefit. When you claim your strengths and lead with them, you'll be better able to see the strengths in others. This is when the magic takes place, relationships transform in positive ways, careers blossom, communication improves, families love each other more, and the world becomes a better place.

Read on, discover your strengths, lead in a manner that brings out the best in others, and enjoy the journey!

The three of you go down the road,
As down the road go you,
the one you know,
the one they see,
and the one you want to be.

——— / / ———

PART 1:
"the one you know"

Part 1 will help you more fully discover the person going down the road that you believe you are, "the one you know." To begin, complete the *INSIGHT Inventory* using the access code on the last page of this book. This will help you identify your personality strengths and explore how these come together to create the fingerprint of the unique and only you.

One of the greatest regrets in life
is being what others would want you to be,
rather than being yourself.
—Shannon L Alder

—//—

Chapter 1

Identifying Your Strengths

Your personality strengths are those traits that you naturally use, are comfortable with, and that seem to flow out of you almost effortlessly. When you use them, you are at your best. You communicate better with work associates, connect easily with friends, parent more skillfully, love others more freely, and come across in a more positive, energetic way.

You'll be quite familiar with some of your traits. They are like old friends who have been with you your entire life. They are part of your identity. When you use them, you'll feel strong, capable, and "in the zone."

However, you may have other strengths that are more difficult to identify. You may sense they are there, a part of you, almost like a shadow. Yet they may not play an active part in your daily behavior. They have been lying dormant, unused perhaps because you may have never fully tapped into them. These are hidden treasures this program will help you uncover.

Strengths from the past

It's also possible that you may need to unearth some personality strengths you do not quite remember that you once had or ones that never emerged. If there were few opportunities to use certain personality traits, they may never have fully developed. Fortunately, they are still there, just waiting for the right conditions to grow and blossom.

Other strengths may have been lost because of negative or critical messages from well-meaning family members, teachers or even friends. The expectations and norms of the setting where you grew up could have influenced you. As a child you were probably a keen observer of what worked when communicating with your family, school instructors, and friends. You also figured out what did not work so well. You probably became very good at modifying your behavior to please others and to stay out of trouble for the most part. In doing this, some of your personality strengths may have been set aside or even lost with time. Now, years later, you may be barely aware of them.

Strengths you may have covered up

When it comes to unleashing your unique personality strengths, you may struggle to see some of them because you intentionally buried them earlier in your life. You probably did this for good reasons; to avoid someone's anger, to escape disapproving comments, or perhaps to fit in. You may have set certain personality strengths aside to survive particular family dynamics. Hopefully those times have changed and now you can bring those strengths out and develop them to their fullest.

Strengths you've developed

Part of what makes you unique comes from personality traits you have developed as you've journeyed though life. It may be that over time you've acquired some strengths that originally did not come naturally. Your ambition and hard work may have helped you to expand your range of behavior on different traits. You may have even switched over to the opposite trait with time and personal growth. This is fairly unusual, but it does occur.

Discover your strengths

It's difficult to fully unleash your strengths until you identify them. This book will help you validate the strengths you are familiar with, find the ones you lost over the years, uncover any hidden ones, and bring them all out into the light to reveal your "true" you. Leading from your strengths will help you lead better.

Knowing yourself is the beginning of all wisdom.

— Aristotle

—//—

Chapter 2

Discovering Yourself

To lead with insight, first you will need to clearly identify your strengths. The *INSIGHT Inventory* will help you begin this journey. You've been provided a website and code in the back of this book. After logging in and completing the assessment, you'll receive a personalized report. The chapters in this book will help you apply this report to leadership and unleash your personality strengths.

Before you start, you may want to learn more about the *INSIGHT Inventory*. The following section describes some of its features and helps you develop a strategy for getting the most out of your report.

If you're ready to complete it, go directly to the website, enter your code, and proceed. When finished, jump to the first page of the next chapter to begin the journey of discovering more about the most interesting person in the world, "you."

About the INSIGHT Inventory

The *INSIGHT Inventory*:

Focuses on strengths

The *INSIGHT Inventory* is strengths-based. It identifies traits that come naturally to you and behaviors that you are good at using. It focuses on positive characteristics and explores ways of expanding and enriching them rather than trying to fix what you do not do so well. The *INSIGHT Inventory* also helps you identify triggers and hot buttons that pull you away from being at your best while providing you with guidance on how to move back to your strengths zone.

Considers the influence of environment

INSIGHT is based on field theory, the premise that your personality and behavior may change depending on the environment or setting you are in. This is why the *INSIGHT Inventory* provides two personality profiles, one for your work behavior, and one for your personal style. This helps you explore what influences your behavior in these settings. It also helps you consider how you may behave in other settings such as on a particular team, around certain family members, or even with a specific person.

Doesn't label or typecast

The *INSIGHT Inventory* uses positive descriptive terms to describe the various trait tendencies. Its primary objective is to help you discover more about yourself and unleash your potential. Therefore, it doesn't use labels, grids, or categories that narrowly define who you are. No labels such as "manager," "teacher," "encourager" are used. Such terms can limit you, sometimes in other people's minds, or worse yet, in your own mind. Type codes and alphabet-soup descriptions are avoided. Rather than restrict you, the *INSIGHT Inventory* will stretch your strengths and expand your potential.

Uses everyday "conversational" language

Since the *INSIGHT Inventory* uses jargon-free, conversational descriptions, you can easily share your results and talk about your traits with others. They will immediately understand what you are saying. The everyday language makes it possible for you to discuss your profiles without having to teach others what certain terminology means. They can ask for clarification without being embarrassed that they don't understand the special phrases, color codes or alphabet acronyms such as those used by other assessments. With clear positive language, conversations move forward more quickly and are more helpful.

Helps you better understand behavior, not predict it

The *INSIGHT Inventory* helps you identify your strengths zone on four personality traits. It does not attempt to predict or lock you into certain job-match formulas. It emphasizes the importance of developing skill at flexing to communicate better so you can succeed in a wide range of career paths. Skill and motivation packaged with personality strength awareness and the ability to flex are the key factors of success; not trying to identify a "perfect" match between your personality and a specific job description. However, if you experience an undue amount of stress at work, the *INSIGHT Inventory* does help you clarify what career paths and relationship interactions continually pull you out of your strengths zone and drain your energy. When you identify these, you can develop plans for finding career matches that don't demand so much flexing.

Allows for change and discovery

You may have a trait that you suppressed earlier in your life because of certain pressures or your sensitivity to the reactions of others. The *INSIGHT Inventory* may help you discover traits and potential strengths you may have lost and have been waiting to reemerge. Sometimes these show up when noticing the differences between your Work Style and Personal Style. Differences generally reveal flexing due to different environmental pressures, but they can also indicate freedom to be yourself in one setting more than the other. Sometimes this can point to strengths that you've suppressed, but now want to unleash and let soar.

Emphasizes the "So what?" question

The "so what" question is key for any self-development program. It asks, "So what do I do with these discoveries about myself, these new insights?" The *INSIGHT Inventory* will help you identify specific behaviors you can change, certain patterns you can eliminate, and important skills you can incorporate into your life to improve communication with others. These, in turn, enhance your relationships at work, school, and home and help you become more of who you want to be.

Identify trait triggers and hot buttons

Trait triggers, sensitive spots, and "hot" buttons cause you to move out of your strengths zone and into problematic, negative behaviors. These can be described as old issues and baggage from the past. Triggers are often self-protective reactions you developed either as a child or adolescent. They probably served to help you avoid conflict, deal with stressful interactions or cope with dysfunctional situations. Now, years later, they may resurface when you are exposed to particular behaviors, comments, or actions. The goal is to become more aware of these triggers, develop some understanding of where they came from, and then intentionally switch to more effective strengths-based responses.

Based on normative and research data

The profiles reveal your scores on scales that provide you with a quick reference to how people in general score. The variable shading from dark to light on each scale simplifies this. An important component of developing "insight" into yourself is learning how your scores compare to population averages. You live and succeed or struggle in groups and organizations. It's important to know where your personality traits fall in comparison to other people. This helps you better understand when to flex and how much to flex to communicate well with others. It also helps you see how unique and special your strengths are.

Takes a different pathway

Personality assessment is an expansive topic and there are many questionnaires, surveys, and tests available to assess its many dimensions. Some assessments identify behaviors, others claim to uncover personality themes or driving motives, still others overlap with identification of values, and some categorize "types" or core tendencies. The results are displayed as codes, scales, themes, type grids, quotients, colors, animal references, and so on. This can get confusing to users and even to psychologists, trainers, and coaches.

The *INSIGHT Inventory* gives you a strengths-focused pathway to discovering your personality traits. It gives you a positive language for discussing how you may be different in various situations and frees you from thinking that you or others are always the same in all situations. It will help you discover and unleash the unique person you are.

Helps you become a "better you"

In addition to helping you identify your personality strengths, the *INSIGHT Inventory* guides you through a process of learning how to become more flexible in your communication skills, increasing your range of effectiveness, reducing conflict with others, eliminating hot buttons and triggers, and in short, becoming a better you.

The better you know yourself, the better your relationship
with the rest of the world.

—Toni Collette

—//—

Chapter 3

Completing the INSIGHT Inventory

The *INSIGHT Inventory* helps you identify your personality strengths. You'll discover your preferences on four traits and how you may behave differently in various environments. You'll also explore the emotional hot buttons and trait triggers that relate to your strongest preferences.

To complete the *INSIGHT Inventory* and obtain your SELF report follow the instructions below:

- Locate your access code in the back of this book
- Go to www.einsightinventory.com
- Enter the code and set up your account.
- Complete the assessment.
- Review your results on screen or print your report.

Once you receive your report, read through it and then return to this book to gain more in-depth insights into your unique personality strengths.

Understand the link between trait intensity and shading.

The location where your scores plot on a trait scale helps explain the intensity of your behavior on that trait. The degree or darkness of shading provides a quick reference. The scores on each scale are plotted on a continuum with a white center zone, two lightly shaded areas, and then two dark shaded areas at either end. The scales look like the image below.

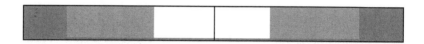

If your score falls in the middle area with no shading, some of the characteristics from both sides of the center line on that scale may describe you.

If your score falls in either the left or right light shaded area, many characteristics of that preference will probably describe you. A few characteristics from the preference on the other side may also fit.

If your score falls in either dark shaded area, most of the characteristics of that preference on that side will describe you.

Therefore, scoring just slightly Direct is quite different from scoring very Direct. Slightly Direct is near the centerline or average for people in general. On the other hand, a very Direct score is much more intense, plots in the dark gray area, and indicates characteristics only 10 percent of the population would exhibit. Another way of saying this is that if you scored in the dark shade on the right hand side, you would be more Direct than 90 percent of people.

Examine your profile shape.

Plotting all four of your scores on a chart creates a profile shape. A profile is generated for both your Work Style and Personal Style. The profiles appear next to each other and comparing them reveals any differences in your trait preferences between work and personal settings. This makes it easy to share your results and discuss the reasons for variations in your behavior.

Example:

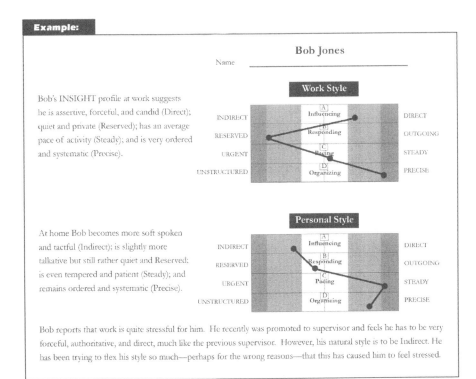

Name _____ Bob Jones

Bob's INSIGHT profile at work suggests he is assertive, forceful, and candid (Direct); quiet and private (Reserved); has an average pace of activity (Steady); and is very ordered and systematic (Precise).

Work Style

INDIRECT — A Influencing — DIRECT
RESERVED — B Responding — OUTGOING
URGENT — C Pacing — STEADY
UNSTRUCTURED — D Organizing — PRECISE

At home Bob becomes more soft spoken and tactful (Indirect); is slightly more talkative but still rather quiet and Reserved; is even tempered and patient (Steady); and remains ordered and systematic (Precise).

Personal Style

INDIRECT — A Influencing — DIRECT
RESERVED — B Responding — OUTGOING
URGENT — C Pacing — STEADY
UNSTRUCTURED — D Organizing — PRECISE

Bob reports that work is quite stressful for him. He recently was promoted to supervisor and feels he has to be very forceful, authoritative, and direct, much like the previous supervisor. However, his natural style is to be Indirect. He has been trying to flex his style so much—perhaps for the wrong reasons—that this has caused him to feel stressed.

Check back at any time.

Your username and password will be saved in the system and you can always return and regenerate your reports. You can also add observers and ask them to rate you from their perspectives. See Part 2 of this book for details on obtaining observer ratings of your personality strengths.

Review your report.

When you first receive your report, flip through it and read the headings and glance through the various charts describing your scores. Then, start again at the beginning and read your report carefully in detail.

There are instructions in some of the sections that ask you to check descriptive phrases. In other areas it is suggested that you mark or prioritize items in bulleted lists. Take the time to complete these activities. They allow you to interact with your report and think through some of the unique aspects of your personality strengths. When sharing your report with others your checkmarks and comments will help you identify some of the descriptions that you'll want to talk about.

Share your report with a friend or co-worker.

You will also learn a lot about yourself by hearing from co-workers, friends, or family members who see your report. They may spot phrases or descriptions of you that have particular meaning to them. They may also identify some terms they don't believe describe you. Sometimes you learn as much hearing what others think "isn't" descriptive of you as you do learning what they think "is" descriptive of you.

Even if you find yourself having different opinions of your behavior, don't try to change their minds, correct them, or debate with them. Their opinions are their own. Respect them and learn from them.

As you review several observer reports, you may notice certain patterns emerging. These can be clues to how you come across in specific situations or around certain people. Its not unusual for a good friend or family member to bring out a side of us that doesn't usually surface. Discussions about these behaviors can be quite interesting and they are undoubtedly important to communication with that person.

Consider special situations.

Also, think about how your behavior may change in some very specific settings. For example, do you behave differently when driving an automobile in rush hour traffic? How does your behavior shift in large groups of people during a meet and greet mixer for business or school? What side of you comes out at large sporting events or concerts? While you may find yourself in these settings only occasionally, the directions your traits tend to move still reveal interesting and unique characteristics about you.

Learn that flexing is the key to communication.

An important section in your report focuses on flexing your behavior to better communicate with others. There are several chapters in this book that expand upon this. The objective is to realize that while your personality is unique and has many embedded strengths; there are other types of strengths. One of these is to be able to intentionally flex your behavior when doing so would help you improve communication with others.

This is easier said than done. Some people know themselves and are proud of their strengths, but want others to do all the adapting and adjusting. Don't be one of those individuals. The better quality involves having insight into your personality traits and be willing to acknowledge that there is a time and place to flex your traits. Your goal is to know yourself well and read others so accurately that you can flex your personality traits at will to improve communication and improve relationships.

Review your results and learn about the traits.

Building a solid core understanding of your strengths is like creating a compass. When you explore the sections on stress reactions, triggers, and hot buttons, having previously identified your strengths on each trait will help you find the direction back home. Some people have trouble doing this. They let their hot buttons misdirect them and they get triggered into negative behaviors and anger outbursts.

These people then get lost and start to see themselves as hot headed or explosive, or out of control. They have trouble getting back to their strengths because they never fully identified them. This is where the phrase "get free" comes from. You'll want to get free from the behaviors that block your success. The best way to do this is point your compass back home to your strengths. The next chapter will get you headed in the right direction

LEAD with INSIGHT

Insight is the ability to go inside yourself and see yourself as others see you.
—Gordon Allport

—//—

Chapter 4

Understanding Trait Strengths

The *INSIGHT Inventory* will help you learn more about your personality traits and how to communicate more successfully with other people. Based on positive psychology, it focuses on your strengths and capacity to flex your style when needed, not on weaknesses. It also helps identify how and why your behavior may shift from one setting to another. When you compare the differences between your Work Style and Personal Style profiles you'll also learn more about your responses to others, stresses you may encounter in each setting, and how you can adapt in ways that keep you in your strengths zone.

The word "INSIGHT"

The word "insight" means to have knowledge of who you are. This requires that you go inside yourself and see what other people see. When you develop a truly accurate perception of how you come across to others, you'll be more tuned into them, and you'll be better able to communicate and build winning relationships.

Having "insight" also means being free of self-deception. This can go one of two ways. There may be certain times that you don't value some of your personality characteristics that others clearly see and really appreciate. This may cause you to downplay and underuse some of your best strengths. At other times, you may feel so proud of a particular trait that you overvalue it and don't realize that it actually has a negative impact on other people.

Just because a trait works for you doesn't mean it wears well with family, friends, and coworkers. Therefore, both undervaluing and overvaluing certain personality traits can reflect poor insight. Good "insight" means that you have developed an accurate perception of yourself. Your *INSIGHT Inventory* self-rating profile and the *Insight Observer Feedback* charts that you will be completing in Part Two will help you compare your self-perception to how others see you.

Start by learning the descriptions

First, get familiar with your self-perception. Learn the descriptions of the four traits and the opposite extremes of each. Your scores indicate ways of behaving you prefer to use most of the time. So develop an in-depth understanding of your traits and a strong vocabulary of self-descriptive terms. Since we live and work in groups, it is also important to build your skill at describing yourself to others.

Try to get away from any preconceived ideas regarding what trait preferences might be desirable and undesirable. Usually if you have a reaction in either way, positive or negative, this indicates you may have a "learned" response. You may have received quite different messages regarding trait characteristics from family, school, your social environment, and other external sources. Your opinion of what is the "best" way to behave may be more theirs than yours. This is the perfect time to build your own perspective.

It can be tough to be tough

Joe's parents were both successful trial attorneys. They were tough-minded, candid, and strong willed. They often brought their intensity and competiveness home with them and even debated and argued around the dinner table. Joe heard over and over from them that he should speak his mind, push back on others who disagreed, and challenge people.

As a team leader in a large organization, he tried to be commanding and forceful but soon learned that this wasn't working for his team and was also very stressful for him. He was innately more indirect and diplomatic and had never developed the strengths of these traits. Now he finds it quite challenging to overcome the old messages, but he is determined to change and be his true self.

Sometimes the larger environment or culture of a particular extended family or ethnic group gives subtle or not so subtle messages about what traits are desirable and undesirable. When you find yourself in new situations you may encounter completely different messages about how to behave. Sometimes these are wonderfully freeing.

Respect your elders

Zoe was raised in a small village in an immigrant neighborhood. Her family continually reminded her to be respectful to elders and authority figures and never argue back or challenge them. This is how it was, they would say, in the old country. Zoe grew up believing that having her own voice or holding her own with older siblings, parents, or family members was wrong and could bring trouble. She learned it was inappropriate to state her opinion if it was different from theirs, raise her voice, or argue back in any way. It simply wasn't okay to be assertive or direct.

These examples show that strong, sometimes biased, messages about personality traits can be learned from the family or childhood environments (school, church, community). Sometimes these support your innate personality tendencies and serve to enhance these traits. At other times, they conflict with your natural strengths. You may develop the belief that you are wrong in expressing these traits and unfortunately, you may struggle to find your true self.

Review the *INSIGHT Inventory* traits. Note, both preferences on each trait are positive and have their strengths.

INDIRECT	[A] **Influencing**	DIRECT
RESERVED	[B] **Responding**	OUTGOING
URGENT	[C] **Pacing**	STEADY
UNSTRUCTURED	[D] **Organizing**	PRECISE

The Four Traits and Their Opposite Preferences

A) Influencing   How you express your thoughts, present ideas, and assert yourself. The opposite preferences are INDIRECT and DIRECT.

B) Responding   How you approach and respond to others, particularly groups of people. The opposite preferences are RESERVED and OUTGOING.

C) Pacing   How quickly you take action and make decisions. The opposite preferences are URGENT and STEADY.

D) Organizing   How you structure your time, carry out projects, and handle details. The opposite preferences are UNSTRUCTURED and PRECISE.

Learn about one trait at a time.

The following four chapters each focus on one trait and its opposite preferences. Each chapter provides detailed descriptions and examples of the trait preferences and characteristics. As you read each chapter, make a note of any differences in behavior between your Work Style and Personal Style profiles. A part of unleashing your strengths involves determining which traits are most descriptive of you in certain environments.

If you notice changes between your Work Style and Personal Style, ask yourself if the differences in your profiles reflect:

- changes due to stressful demands either at work (school) or home.
- temporary style changes due to certain unexpected pressures or short-term stresses.
- learned skills, intentional flexing of your style that helps you communicate better with certain people in your life.

You'll find that some of the changes will reflect the influence and impact of the environment. The temporary changes are fairly easy to deal with. You'll learn strategies for identifying what is impacting you and how to make plans for either adapting or eventually moving away from these pressures.

The long-term changes that are due to chronic stress are more difficult to spot, but they are really important to diagnose. These are the times you're being someone you aren't. Sometimes this has gone on for so long that you've lost track of your true personality strengths. These long-term stress adaptations can lead to dissatisfaction with life, low-grade depression, even physical illness. It will be important to identify these shifts, track them over time, and create a strategy for change that you can aspire to and that will release joy rather than stress.

This brings us back to the starting point—identifying, understanding, and fully owing your strengths. Knowledge of each of the four traits, their tendencies, and the embedded strengths will get you headed in the right direction. The next chapters will take you there.

Speak clearly, if you speak at all; carve every word before you let it fall.
— Oliver Wendell Holmes, Sr.

Too many of us fail to fulfill our needs because we say no rather than yes, and yes when we should say no.
— William Glasser

—//—

Chapter 5

Scale A: Influencing

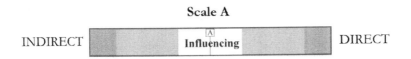

Scale A identifies how you express your thoughts, present your opinions, and assert yourself. This scale measures the manner in which you voice your positions on issues and how you convey your thoughts and ideas. The two opposite preferences, Indirect and Direct, identify two opposite ways of communicating with and influencing others.

Oops, sorry I said that!

Laura, a very Direct division manager, states her opinions quickly and candidly. She admits that she's had to apologize for things she's said or at least how she said them. At the time she said them, she felt she was just being honest and presenting the facts as she saw them; describing reality as it was. But, Laura admits that sometimes she doesn't think through how her comments come across to others. She doesn't intend to hurt anyone's feelings. However, she does warn team members that if they ask for her opinion, she'll give it. She's found that it works well with some people, but not with others.

No conflict please

Ken is Indirect. He tries to get along and avoid conflict in all of his relationships. He is very careful about what he says and how he says it. If you ask him for his opinion, he will try to be as diplomatic as possible and give a measured answer that doesn't create tension or hard feelings. Sometimes others aren't clear where he stands on an issue, but he would rather clarify his position later than take the chance of creating a heated argument. His co-workers like his tactful manner, but his strong-minded manager often treats him as if he were invisible.

Both individuals in the examples may be successful in influencing others in positive ways and they may both be good leaders of their work teams and family groups. However, they will come across quite differently. The Indirect and Direct preferences each have their strengths and advantages in certain situations. When you look at your score, focus on the positive characteristics, but stay open to understanding how they could be interpreted differently by others.

Locate your score on Scale A

Take a look at your results and identify whether you scored more toward the Indirect or Direct side.

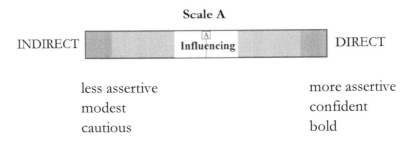

less assertive   more assertive
modest   confident
cautious   bold

INDIRECT

Descriptions of the INDIRECT Preference:

You influence others using strategy and diplomacy.

If you scored to the left of the centerline on Scale A, you use the Indirect preference when influencing others. You state your positions on issues with caution and tact, being sensitive to the needs and desires of others. You avoid overstating your opinions and phrase comments carefully and tentatively to avoid offending or upsetting people. When expressing how you feel about something, you tend to present your position diplomatically. Sometimes you may even do this so carefully that it becomes difficult for others to get a clear sense of where you stand.

When she speaks, people listen

Kylee is a leader on her team, but she is so soft spoken that few people would guess she is in charge. She seldom raises her voice and no one has ever heard her get demanding. However, when she speaks everyone listens. When she wants something done, she makes a clear, but polite request. If she is unhappy with the progress of a project, she diplomatically presents her concerns and helps focus on the problem, not the person. Rarely is she involved in a conflict or agitated debate. She says she "leads from behind."

You influence others with a supportive and tactful approach.

When persuading others, you prefer to carefully introduce ideas and build your case, rather than presenting your opinions boldly and directly. By expressing your thoughts with tact, you convert others to your viewpoint, often without causing them to feel the need to challenge your position. They might even find themselves believing that your ideas are their ideas, because your subtle influence has gently eased them into agreeing with you.

"We" need to take "our" medicine now

Carrie is the evening care attendant in a pediatric wing of a hospital. Getting young patients to take their medicine is a daily challenge. Carrie's success is legendary and she is often asked to work with children who are defiant and resisting their meds. Carrie would seem to be the least likely to be able to accomplish this. Most charge nurses believe they need to call in someone who can be direct and firm.

However, Carrie is just the opposite; she is very soft-spoken and almost tentative in her requests. After she meets the children and gently requests the medicine be taken and presented all the funny and interesting reasons why it's a good idea, most of the patients readily comply. They even take credit for being such willing and wise patients. Somehow she flips the situation and her requests become their ideas

You come across as approachable and unassuming.

As an Indirect person, it will be easy for others to approach and talk with you. Since you typically don't take a hard and firm stance on issues, others will freely share their perspective and offer their ideas and counter-opinions. This is not to say you don't have strong opinions, you just tend to downplay them, at least at first.

Your unassuming style means you don't present your positions in ways that imply that they are absolutely correct or set in stone. This characteristic helps you present some fairly strong opinions in ways that don't cause others to challenge them. You often use language that takes the edge off your position. For example, you may open with phrases such as: "Perhaps another way to look at this is..." or "I wonder if..." or "I'm not absolutely sure about this, but..." etc.

Be aware that your unassuming approach may work against you at times. Others, particularly very direct assertive individuals, may believe your tactful style indicates that you lack confidence in your ideas. They may think you're unsure of yourself when you begin your statements with questions. Your diplomatic style can trigger others to talk over you or discount your points. So be prepared to be more emphatic or direct when needed. A famous quote is "walk softly, but carry a big stick."

Creative, but invisible

Kenny is Indirect and gets along with everyone on his team. He rarely says things that offend others. But, sometimes Kenny can't figure out why his creative ideas are not taken seriously. He's careful to not come across as arrogant and downplays how terrific he believes his new ideas are. He often describes them as "just something he was thinking about" or "a plan that might or might not work." But, some co-workers don't seem to hear him or give him time to finish when he does this. He realizes the problem is not the quality of his ideas, but rather the way he presents them and has vowed to learn how to be more assertive in those situations.

You prefer to negotiate rather than argue or debate differences.

The give and take of debating issues sometimes requires diplomacy (which you're probably good at) and at other times, taking a firm stand and strongly presenting your position. As an Indirect person, you'd prefer to avoid having to be forceful and strong willed. You would rather politely discuss the pros and cons of each side. Even when you have strong convictions, you may present them somewhat tentatively. When discussing your positions and beliefs on an issue, one strategy is to be firm in principle, but use tactful non-threatening language to get your points across.

You tend to "ask" rather than "tell."

When you want something done, you will tend to use an "asking" rather than a "telling" style to influence others to take action. For example, you may ask: "Can you finish this…?" or "Would you mind closing that door…?" and "Could you get such and such…?" Asking for what you want softens the request and fits your preference for diplomacy and conflict avoidance. An "asking" style can be very effective, particularly with other Indirect individuals and in situations where emotions are running high. However, there may be times when others might not realize that your question is meant as a directive and you may feel ignored or ineffective.

Did I make that clear?

Carly is very tactful and diplomatic and the other teachers in her math department selected her as their new team leader. She rarely offends anyone and she is modest and always asks for ideas and assistance rather than demanding input. However, her Indirect style is sometimes unclear to some of the new team members. They do better when they know exactly what lesson plans to complete, how to do these properly, and when to turn them in. In those situations, Carly really has to flex her style to be more frank and use more directive language to keep them from getting lost.

You present new ideas modestly, sometimes understating them.

You tend to understate your ideas, their benefits, and downplay how you came up with them. Even if you believe a recent idea you came up with is particularly good, you may modify your delivery and say something like, "Now this may not be much..." or "I was just thinking..." This modest approach can at times help you introduce ideas to people who might otherwise be closed off to input. On the other hand, there is a risk that your ideas may be discounted by others, particularly more Direct individuals, because the way you present them doesn't come across confident and forceful enough.

Your strengths include:

Mediating and facilitating discussions by keeping your own issues in the background.

Your strengths include your ability to modestly hold back your ideas and facilitate group discussion and your ability to mediate conflict. Since you dislike conflict, you're motivated to help reduce it when it surfaces among others. Because you are good at keeping your own issues low-key and in the background, you probably make a very effective mediator. You can tactfully urge others to bring forth their ideas and discuss their feelings. You are naturally good at not interrupting others and instead, asking questions to explore and probe each individual's position more deeply. You try not to cut anyone's dialogue off prematurely and encourage discussion by listening to and validating everyone's ideas often above your own or at least in addition to your own ideas.

Phrasing comments carefully so you don't offend others or create conflict.

Your tendency to focus on the needs and positions of other people allows you to get along well with them. Just as being Indirect implies, you're careful to phrase ideas in ways that don't offend others. The cautious phrasing of your comments creates a safe space for conversation. A strength of your Indirect preference is that you maintain relationships by minimizing undue tension or unnecessary conflicts.

How You Walk Your Walk

Certain body language behaviors, patterns, and cues are characteristic of Indirect individuals. Some of these include:
- hesitant or fleeting eye contact
- soft voice tone
- non-intrusive body language, i.e. standing back at a distance
- gentle handshake, even when firm
- hesitant expressions, tentative gestures

How You Talk Your Talk

- *Joe, when you get a chance will you help me out with this project?*
- *Mary, please finish up this work when you get a chance.*
- *Could you take it over there the first chance you get?*
- *I'm not completely sure, but I believe this will work.*

Possible Mottos:

- Avoid conflict at all cost.
- Turn the other cheek.

DIRECT

Descriptions of the DIRECT preference:

You influence others using assertiveness and conviction.

If you scored to the right of the centerline on Scale A, you prefer to use a Direct style of influencing others. The further to the right your score is, the more intensely you'll exhibit this preference. As a Direct person, when communicating with others, you state your positions candidly in a very straightforward manner. When trying to get your ideas across and accepted, you are assertive and convincing. When striving to get results, you approach tasks, projects, and those involved with willfulness and conviction.

The following characteristics will tend to describe you:

You state your position on issues candidly and frankly.

As a Direct individual you are frank and forthright when you present your opinions, thoughts, and ideas. You come across very convincing and self-assured in conversations or meetings. Others will know exactly where you stand. You state your speculations and new ideas in the same confident manner and sometimes others may assume you know exactly what you're talking about, even when you are actually just seeking further discussion and feedback.

You may at times say things so forcefully that your comments come across as brusque or critical and you inadvertently hurt other's feelings. You may not intend to do so, but when you focus on tasks rather than people, your words may come out as non-caring.

You influence others with an assertive, direct approach.

When you strive to convince or influence others, you use a confident strong-willed approach. You'll tend to come across as "in charge" and somewhat domineering. These attributes can be positive, particularly when others seek your leadership and want your advice. However, these same characteristics can be perceived negatively when others feel you are overstepping your authority. If you're a parent or work with children you've probably heard the retort, "You're not the boss of me!" from a young person who is resisting your directives.

Taking charge

When there is confusion in the work group, people often turn to Mark because he is so good at cutting through any confusion to the key issues and assertively taking charge. He can be blunt, but at times this is somewhat reassuring and helps get everyone back on track. However, when an open discussion and consideration of every ones' ideas are needed, Mark's forceful style doesn't work as well. He is rather intimidating and sometimes people are hesitant to speak up because they think he will challenge or even argue with them.

You come across as self-assured and forceful.

When stating your thoughts, you come across as very self-assured and solidly convinced. Your air of confidence can be persuasive, particularly at those times when there is confusion around issues, upcoming deadlines, or emergencies. You may even sound convinced of a course of direction or position, even when you really aren't so certain of the best pathway yourself.

You prefer to confront conflicts and openly debate differences.

You rarely back away from conflicts or arguments, preferring to confront differences in opinions head on. Since you like getting issues out in the open, you probably enjoy a good debate and the occasional heated exchange. The back-and-forth jousting serves as a way for you to test other people's convictions and even clarify your own positions.

Running into the fire

People say that when there are fires or conflicts, Lucy runs toward them. She enjoys challenging other peoples' ideas, sometimes even when she agrees with them. She just wants to see if they will stand up for themselves. In her mind, if people won't fight for their ideas they don't really feel strongly enough about them. This is not always the case, but Lucy's co-workers and friends learn to hold their ground, not back down, and never take her intense questioning personally.

You tend to "tell" rather than "ask."

You use a telling language that often makes your calls for action and requests sound like directives and commands. For example, if you want a chair moved, you might say, "Mary, move that chair to the other side of the room." Or, perhaps more politely, but still emphatically, "Please move that chair." By comparison, Indirect people tend to form their request as questions and their tone of voice will be more hesitant with a tentative quality to it.

If people don't want to know what you think, they probably shouldn't ask because you'll usually come right out and tell them! This frankness, what you might label as "honesty," works for you at times and can be problematic in other situations.

You present ideas with confidence, sometimes overstating them.

When you state ideas or your position on issues, you'll convey confidence and conviction. You'll tend to err on the side of overstatement, rather than understatement. Your confidence comes out in the tone of voice and the selection of adjectives you use. It's not unusual for you to use such emphatic words as "always," "never," and "absolutely," among others. This direct, self-assured manner can be very convincing to others and it can help uncover opposing ideas quickly.

When confidence works, and when it doesn't

Dave, a mid-level manager, was so direct and convincing that he talked his entire work team into moving ahead on an idea before it had been tested. Since it was a great marketing opportunity, and he actually was correct, his team was appreciative of his conviction. On the other hand, some members remember incident months ago where he convinced them that the "right" way to travel to a marketing event was by taking a route that only he knew. He was so wrong, having remembered it incorrectly, that everyone got lost and missed the meeting entirely. Team members learned that just because Dave sounds convincing, doesn't mean he is always correct.

Your strengths include:

Taking charge, especially in situations that need control and clear direction.

Using your Direct preference, you're very good at moving in and taking charge in ambiguous or chaotic situations. In these instances, your frank, forceful style is actually welcomed because people are seeking answers and an end to the confusion. When time is of the essence, assertive take-charge leadership is often the best option. You are talented at establishing command and gaining support in situations that have spiraled out of control.

Getting vague or hidden issues out on the table and restated in a bottom-line, straightforward way.

Since you are willing to confront issues head on, you often push for the frank and open discussion of issues. You're not afraid to address the hidden issues, the "elephant in the room," and get people to acknowledge the obvious. You work best when everyone lays their cards on the table. However, while people want the truth, they differ in how bluntly they want it delivered. If you're helping a group of people solve a problem, you may find that some participants do not cope well with your candid, plainspoken approach and need it softened a bit.

Conflict? No problem!

Katrina is known for two characteristics. The first is her ability to step back and observe situations and see what is going on underneath the surface. The second is being bold and assertive enough to stop everything and push others to talk about any hidden issues. Katrina has little or no fear of conflict. She actually believes it's a good thing. Teams and groups she is a member of quickly learn that she is direct and always striving to get interpersonal issues out in the open before they cause bigger problems later. Even though this often makes people uncomfortable, they appreciate her forthright style.

How you walk your walk

You probably display many of these behaviors:

- Direct eye contact—you look people in the eye and like to receive this in return
- Strong convincing tone of voice— strong, and occasionally a bit intimidating
- Upright, proud posture
- Forceful handshake and greeting gestures
- Unwavering, at times rather intense, facial expression
- Strong emphatic gestures such as finger pointing and waving
- Confident, often bigger than life presence

How You Talk Your Talk

When wanting others to do something, you'll tell others candidly what you want and will do so in a commanding manner.

- *Joe, come over here and help me with this project.*
- *Mary, get this work done ... please!*
- *Move that crane to the other site right now.*
- *This will work!*
- *This is absolutely the best way to do it.*

Mottos:

Move on over, I'm coming through.
Don't push unless you want me to push back.
If you want the truth, be sure you can handle the truth.

What Scale A is NOT

Not a measure of success.

Scale A, is an indicator of your style of influencing others; it describes your approach, not the outcomes. An Indirect person can be just as influential as a Direct person. Influence is most strongly impacted by people's authority, experience, and position. A powerful, Indirect person could influence a group of people just as much or more than a Direct individual. Direct people may sound convincing, but if they are outsiders to a group or inexperienced then they will have little influence. Scale A is a measure of the approach and tactics that people use, not an indication of their success.

Not a measure of confidence.

You can be confident in your abilities regardless of whether you are Indirect or Direct. A confident, Indirect person comes across as quietly self-assured, while a confident Direct person comes across as boldly self-assured. You can use either tactful diplomacy or candid assertiveness to present your ideas. Both can work.

Not a measure of assertiveness.

Both Indirect and Direct people can be assertive. They both can declare, present, and affirm their positions in a clear and confident manner. However, when forcefulness is needed, Direct individuals can more easily come across as frank and strong than Indirect individuals. When tactfulness, and an unassuming manner is appropriate, Indirect people can more easily display these traits.

Not a measure of power.

Power comes from experience, position within an organization, intelligence, and acquired knowledge. People defer power to others either by respecting their experience and character or by accepting the title and position they hold. Powerful people can be either Indirect or Direct; however, they wield their power differently and their style will be related to their preference for influencing with either Direct or Indirect behaviors.

Not a measure of self-esteem.

Due to their candid, bold manner of presenting their positions, Direct individuals are often perceived as self-confident. However, an Indirect person can be self-assured and confident too. This works the other way, also. A Direct person's frank and straightforward manner can disguise insecurity and doubt, while an Indirect person's sensitive expression can belie their expert knowledge and confidence.

Cultural and gender differences

Statistically men and women score about the same. The normative data is very similar, so much so that the statistical data points were merged. Both genders plot their results on the same scales. However, there remain certain stereotypes and cultural biases to take into consideration. Many women who score Direct find that they have to be cautious in displaying candor, bluntness, and straightforwardness in many work and culturally framed settings. While men can exhibit these behaviors and be labeled strong and forceful, women often get labeled as pushy, difficult, and bossy. This bias appears to be slowly changing, but it is still prevalent in many organizations and regional subcultures.

There are also biases between large cultures. For example, as a generality, in the United States and many western European countries it is considered desirable to be Direct and assertive. In East Asian and Pacific Rim countries, Indirectness and deference to others, particularly elders, is thought of as the more respectful and honorable characteristic.

Summary Worksheet–Scale A, Influencing

To create a quick summary of your preferences on this trait check (√) the phrases that best describe your Work Style. Then, to highlight differences in your behavior at home, place an **X** next to the traits that fit your Personal Style.

Scale A: Influencing

INDIRECT: You influence others using strategy and diplomacy and:

____ State your position on issues carefully and diplomatically

____ Persuade others with a supportive and tactful approach.

____ Come across as approachable and unassuming.

____ Prefer to negotiate rather than argue or debate differences.

____ Prefer to "ask" rather than "tell."

____ Present new ideas modestly, sometimes understating them.

OR

DIRECT: You express yourself with assertiveness, conviction, and:

____ State your position on issues candidly and frankly.

____ Influence others with an assertive, direct approach.

____ Come across as self-assured and forceful.

____ Prefer to confront conflicts and openly debate differences.

____ Tend to "tell" rather than "ask."

____ Present ideas with confidence, sometimes overstating them.

The wind howls, but the mountain remains still.
— Japanese Proverb

To deprive a gregarious creature of companionship is to maim it,
to outrage its nature.
— John Wyndham

— / / —

Chapter 6

Scale B: Responding

Scale B

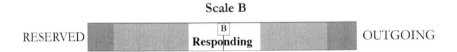

RESERVED   **Responding**   OUTGOING

Scale B measures how you respond to others, particularly groups of people, and it describes your level of talkativeness, expressiveness, and sociability. Your score indicates the way you move toward people, express your emotions, and interact. The two opposite preferences are Reserved and Outgoing. If you scored Reserved, you'll tend to be rather quiet and self-contained. If you scored Outgoing, you'll be expressive, talkative, and open.

Scale B assesses your responsiveness to people and the manner in which you connect and establish your relationships with others. If you are a Reserved person, you tend respond to people with a quiet, introspective style and you'll prefer interacting with others one-on-one rather than in large groups. You probably hold back and do not say much during group discussions, particularly when in large meetings. However, you may talk openly when alone with a single individual and with close friends, or when in very small groups of people.

If you are an Outgoing person, you'll respond to others with open exchanges of emotion, expressiveness, and animation. You'll enjoy groups, often the larger the better, and get energized by the energy they bring. The sounds of people talking, the rising inflections of humor and playfulness will be stimulating to you and you'll fall into the cadence and flow of the group interactions.

Try not to generalize. Reserved people can often be warm and friendly and Outgoing people can sometimes be cool and distant. Neither preference is more desirable than the other. As you review the characteristics of this scale, keep in mind it is about the number of the relationships people prefer and how they express themselves in those relationships.

Locate your score on Scale B

Take a look at your results and identify whether you scored more toward the Reserved or Outgoing side.

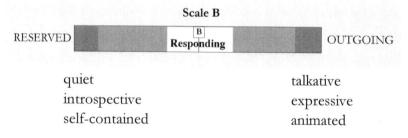

RESERVED

Descriptions of the RESERVED Preference:

You are most at ease interacting with others one–on–one.

As a Reserved person, the size of the group you are in makes a difference. You tend to be more comfortable approaching and talking with others either one-on-one or in small groups. You will probably be hesitant to speak up freely in group settings or large meetings unless you are in a position of authority or have some positional status. Even then, you'll say things with as few of words as possible rather than talking excessively. Generally, you prefer conversations with people, one individual at a time or in small groups of two or three.

You keep your emotions rather private and self-contained.

As a Reserved person, you'll tend to share less information about yourself than Outgoing individuals do. This is particularly true when it comes to sharing personal emotions, which you'll most likely keep to yourself. During the infrequent times you do reveal your emotions, it will be only with people you know quite well. When you talk, you will tend to speak about places, objects, or things rather than your feelings or relationships with other people.

When you are asked how you are feeling, you are likely to answer by describing what you are thinking or what recently happened, rather than what you're feeling. You've even probably developed skill at avoiding questions about your feelings. Others who interact with you need to be prepared to be patient, build their relationship with you first, and probe politely until a relationship is formed. This may cause others to find you a bit difficult to get to know at first.

A closed book on feelings

Darrel's supervisor says she never knows how he is feeling. Since she knows his wife, Stacy, sometimes she will ask her. But, Stacy says she doesn't know either. Most of Darrel's friends describe him as pleasant and friendly, however when asked more about him, they realize they don't really talk much. Darrel is Reserved and very private and while he engages in warm conversations, mostly by being a good listener, he doesn't share much about himself. He typically deflects questions about his feelings or emotions and switches topics and keeps his feelings private. Darrel is well liked but a bit of a mystery to those who try to get to know him.

You get energized when alone and away from activity.

As a Reserved person, you recharge and re-energize best when away from people and activity. Too much stimulation is stressful and detracts from your thoughts and concentration. Since you tend to focus internally on your thoughts and ideas, you need time to turn inwardly, away from external noise and activity. You reenergize by being alone for extended times. In contrast, Outgoing people get energized when around others. The more talking, music, and noise, the more alert and energized they become. For you, this works just the opposite way. When around people for too long, you begin to feel drained and a bit overwhelmed and you'll soon seek out time alone to recover.

Janis looks for the back door

Janis is frequently asked to office luncheons. She travels a lot and has an interesting career that others like to hear about. Although she is Reserved, she always enjoys meeting new co-workers and chatting a bit. However, it doesn't take long before she is ready to leave. If the group wants to stay and continue their meeting she'll retreat back to her office for a one-on-one conversation with someone. She's not trying to be aloof; she just gets "peopled" out quickly and needs her time away from meetings with groups. She's even been known to quietly say goodbye and leave unnoticed through a back door. She's a bit uncomfortable with attention, networking, and small talk.

You prefer to think problems through alone to clarify feelings.

When it comes to identifying and clarifying feelings people tend to follow one of two patterns, either "thinking things out" or "talking issues out." As a Reserved person, you fall into the "think it out" category. When overwhelmed with information and mixed feelings, you'll prefer to have alone time to think through the issues and slowly clarify your feelings. After taking the needed time to do this, you will usually be in a much better position to describe your emotions to others and discuss solutions and alternatives to any recent issues.

When you, as a Reserved person, want time to think things out privately, an Outgoing co-worker, friend, or family member may notice you sitting alone and think that you might be lonely or feeling left out. In other situations, Outgoing people may take your need for alone time personally, believing that you don't want to be with them. Be sure to let them know you are just enjoying your alone time.

You use few gestures and facial expressions when you talk.

Your tendency to use very few and fairly subtle facial expressions when you talk makes it difficult for others, particularly Outgoing individuals, to identify your feelings and emotions. If you're an extremely Reserved individual, you may not display many physical clues about what you're thinking or feeling. This does not mean you lack emotions—it's just that you do not tend to show them publicly. When you do, you'll probably do so in a hard-to-read, rather controlled manner. You will smile rather than laugh, tear up rather than cry, and frown a little rather than get upset.

The mask.

Carl is a pleasant manager, but others find him very hard to read. He just doesn't show much emotion. Happy, mad, glad, sad, his expression barely changes. Sometimes when his secretary asks him if he's having a good day he'll answer "yes," and she always responds with the quip, "Then tell your face." and she has a big laugh. She sees his kind hard-working side and isn't put off by his quiet reserved style. He has learned to enjoy the good natured teasing.

You contact friends and acquaintances only occasionally.

As a Reserved person, when it comes to contacting friends and acquaintances, you'll tend to be less active than Outgoing individuals. You may feel that a text message or two, an occasional social media check-in, or possible phone call every couple of months is perfectly adequate for maintaining relationships and friendships. Your Reserved friends and family may feel the same way and be perfectly comfortable with those infrequent contacts. However, this infrequent contact can frustrate Outgoing individuals. They tend to relate to others through more frequent interactions and updates. When they do not hear from you, they may interpret this as indifference and think that you don't care about them. Be sure to find ways to remind yourself to initiate contact with others, at least on important events and holidays.

Your strengths include:

Listening intently and letting others talk more than you.

Your willingness to listen and your low need to talk gives others the space and time to discuss their issues. You can be a wonderful sounding board for others and a great balance for their need to talk through issues. Whether you are their friend, co-worker or family member, Outgoing people often find the difference between their high need to talk and your willingness to listen to be an ideal match.

Keeping information hidden by facial expressions and emotions.

Since you display few facial or body language cues and you do not tend to talk excessively, you can be quite good at safekeeping confidential information. You may even find that you can put this characteristic to good use when negotiating because you hold your cards close to your chest (a phrase for the ability to not show emotional expression) and you do not give out many clues about what you are thinking.

How You Walk Your Walk

You most likely

- use few gestures
- have rather closed body language
- are somewhat uncomfortable touching and hugging others

How You Talk Your Talk

You'll say things with few words and even fewer superlatives.

- *Nice idea, Mary.*
- *It sounds like a reasonable solution, Joe.*
- *Combining a business meeting with a sports event sounds exhausting. Let's meet in a small quiet venue.*

Mottos:

- The sound of silence.
- Quiet please!

OUTGOING

Descriptions of the OUTGOING Preference

If you score Outgoing on Scale B, you are talkative, animated, and very expressive; you're a "people person." You enjoy others and feel particularly comfortable in groups. You respond to others with an open, expressive manner.

You are at ease interacting with many people and groups.

As an Outgoing individual, you like people and want to be liked in return. Involvement with groups energizes you. You connect with others using warmth, expressive interactions, and an animated sense of humor. It is very likely you have an inviting smile, easy-to-read facial expressions, and a contagious laugh. These draw others to you and help you meet and make new friends readily.

Always time to say "hello"

When making rounds in the hospital, Dr. Rod as he's affectionately called, always seems to find someone he can talk to, joke around with, or give a big hug. Even when he is dealing with emergencies and in a hurry, he greets others warmly. People seem to be drawn to him and want to work with him. However, he says it's just because he likes others and truly enjoys people. He makes it a point to say hello, express genuine interest, and make connections. His Outgoing nature has won him many loyal team members and friends.

You share emotions openly and freely.

As an Outgoing person you will tend to be open and share much of your world and your experiences with others. If you are happy, mad, glad, or sad, you will probably express this to others. Since you are fairly transparent with your feelings, others can easily read them. Friends and acquaintances might say you tend to wear your emotions on your sleeve. This makes it easy for others, even new acquaintances, to connect with you and celebrate or commiserate with you, almost as if they have known you for a long time.

You get energized by people contact and lots of activity.

People, activity, and music will energize you. Even if you're rather tired or burned out, when you join a group where there's lots of joking, talking, and activity, you will end up re-energized. By contrast, many Reserved individuals in the same situation would find themselves even more drained and fatigued. As an Outgoing person, you will tend to take in external sources of energy such as music and noise and use this to build your own. You probably do well in meet-and-greet situations where there are people you know, and new individuals to meet.

You may find that with your high need for energy and stimulation, you get bored and tune out unless you find the opportunity to talk or discuss issues with others. It's the interaction and contact that helps you stay energized and interested. Likewise, classes and training sessions that lack opportunities for group discussion can be quite boring for you.

Prefer to talk problems out with others to clarify feelings.

You connect with others through emotion, feelings, and relationships. Because you're a "people person," you notice what's happening with others and become concerned when something goes wrong with interpersonal relationships. Your focus is more on the relationship dynamics, rather than the task or project. You put your thoughts into words and closely note the interactions and feelings of those you're communicating with. This helps you connect with them and unravel your own perspectives on things. Until you've had a chance to fully discuss your observations and feelings, you may not be receptive to solutions offered, no matter how good those solutions might be.

> ### Talking in order to think.
>
> Mickey is very Outgoing. When she arrives at work, she wants to talk out the day's issues. Discussing what went well the day before or problems that may come up gives her a way to sort the day out and clarify her feelings. When co-workers interrupt and try to solve problems, it throws her off. She is looking more for connection and reflection. For her, talking is a way of dissipating stress and planning ahead. Once she has had time to talk things out, she usually comes up with her own solutions to the challenges at hand.

Use lots of gestures and facial expressions when you talk.

As an Outgoing person, you'll tend to be fairly animated and expressive when you talk. You'll use many hand gestures and very expressive body language. If your hands were tied behind your back, you'd probably feel like you just couldn't fully share your feelings You may even catch yourself reaching out and touching other peoples' arms or shoulders as you emphasize points. This reflects your ease and comfort with people and your focus on making contact when communicating.

Contact friends and acquaintances frequently.

As an Outgoing individual, you're fairly good at maintaining many contacts and friendships. Not all of these are necessarily close personal friends, but they are all part of a wide circle of relationships, acquaintances, and contacts you have. This doesn't happen accidentally; friendships grow when properly cared for and attended to and this comes naturally to you. You'll keep track of the events in others lives (birthdays, anniversaries, graduations, marriages, etc.) and reach out in some way, perhaps calling, sending notes or using social media to make quick online contact.

Your strengths include:

Being good at meeting and greeting others, putting them at ease, and making them feel important.

You have your "people" antennae extended and are ever conscious of others who come into your circle of influence. When you notice others, you usually do something about it. You will initiate contact, introduce yourself, and open up communications. You tend to be very good at speaking first, but also saying and doing things that put others at ease. Plus, you're probably a great connecter; you think of people others might enjoy meeting and find ways to get them together, with or without you. You enjoy the process of building relationships.

Staying connected and up to date on personal issues that others may be going through.

Since you are people-oriented, not only do you maintain lots of contacts with others, you usually stay up-to-date on what is happening in other's lives. You ask personal questions and inquire into people's lives. Since you're interested in others and also their relationships, you'll find out how people are doing and you'll remember the relationship dynamics. That is how you stay connected with people. Some of your friends or family may even come to you to find out what's going on in the lives of mutual friends, rather than asking those friends themselves!

How You Walk Your Walk

You'll tend to use:

- lots of gestures
- open body language when talking and greeting others
- touch, hugging, and physical contact reaching out to others.

How You Talk Your Talk

You'll say things enthusiastically and with lots of superlatives:

- *Mary, your idea is absolutely wonderful! I love it!*
- *I can't wait to try this Joe. You're great! You've answered all my problems.*
- *Honey, this vacation with our friends will be incredible! There will be so many activities. It'll be fun!*

Motto:

- People who love people.
- The more the merrier.
- People make the world go round.

What Scale B is Not

Not a measure of shyness

Being Reserved doesn't mean you are shy. Being Outgoing doesn't mean you are confident in all social settings. Reserved individuals are fairly quiet but that is not the same as social shyness. Shyness is related to confidence in groups, social experience, and sometimes self-esteem. Reserved people who are self-assured and confident will often remain quiet in large groups simply because they prefer keeping their thoughts to themselves, not because they are afraid to speak up. In small gatherings of friends or co-workers, some Reserved individuals will actually come across quite talkative and expressive. The true test is to observe how they behave in large groups where there are strangers to meet and greet; usually they will pull back to their more Reserved behavior.

Some very Outgoing people are quite shy around strangers or when in groups with different expertise or experience (business professionals, different age groups, the other gender, etc.) If Outgoing people feel left out they can be very shy. It's also worth noting that an Outgoing person who has low self-esteem or is uncomfortable around certain people (strangers or authority figures, for instance) may not speak up and can also come across as quite shy.

Not a rating of the ability to talk

When explaining their behavior, many Reserved individuals say they just don't feel like talking; therefore, they don't. They see this as a choice they are making and a behavior pattern they have developed, not a confidence or self-esteem issue.

Even though they are Reserved, they may be quite articulate and skilled at social interactions. Some Reserved individuals are quite at ease around others, but just choose to remain rather quiet. They may even enjoy interacting with certain groups of friends, hobbyists, or career specialty areas. They may talk a lot about topics that they are very knowledgeable about, such as a particular interest area or life experience, but that's not the same as connecting with people. When it comes to relationship dynamics Reserved individuals will be less talkative and engaged with people in large unfamiliar groups.

Not an indicator of interest in people

Outgoing people usually look forward to being around others; they enjoy the interactions, the dynamics, and the laughter. They get more energized, hyped up, and engaged when in groups. Reserved people are more cautious in joining groups, but they can enjoy them if they know that the gatherings are not going to go on too long and they will be with people they know. Reserved individuals go into social situations aware that it's going to consume energy on their part. Outgoing people go in anticipating that their energy is going to be amped up and fueled by the interactions.

Group burnout comes at different time periods for Reserved and Outgoing people. Reserved individuals get over stimulated more quickly when around groups, noise, and stimuli. Even when they look forward to joining certain groups, they don't last long. They are soon looking for an escape or cut the interactions short. Outgoing individuals on the other hand, can cope with the stimulation from groups much longer. They thrive on conversations, and may even stay in the groups longer than they originally intended.

Not a measure of persuasiveness

Occasionally businesses make hiring decisions based on false stereotypes. They may believe that only Outgoing people make good sales representatives. These businesses fail to take into account the type of situation the sales representatives will need to work in and the customer types they are selling to. Consequently, these companies often screen out Reserved individuals and try to pick only Outgoing applicants. This can be a mistake. Some Reserved individuals can make great sales representatives, particularly if they work one-to-one with clients. In these situations, Reserved people can even outperform very Outgoing counterparts. Assuming product knowledge, experience, and confidence are equal, a Reserved sales representative who is working one-to-one with a customer, perhaps even over the phone or by online video-streaming, may be perceived as a better listener, warmer and more personable than an Outgoing, very talkative sales representative.

On the other hand, Reserved individuals tend not to enjoy sales positions where they have to do a great deal of meeting, greeting, building new relationships, and presenting of products and services to groups. This doesn't mean they can't do an excellent job if they are trained in presentation skills and highly motivated, but it probably indicates they won't enjoy that part of a sales position that requires those behaviors as much as an extremely Outgoing person would.

Not a measure of warmth

It is sometimes believed that since Outgoing people are friendly and talkative, they are "warmer" than Reserved individuals. However, interpersonal warmth or coolness is an inner value rather than the behavior assessed by this scale. Reserved people can be open, caring, and warm, but still come across as quiet and soft-spoken. On the other hand, some Outgoing individuals can appear to be very friendly, but still be a bit indifferent, disinterested in others, and interpersonally cool. Scale B assesses the behavior, not the driving motives and energy behind the behavior. Don't equate either Outgoing or Reserved preferences with personal values or interpersonal warmth and caring.

Not an indicator of confidence

Even as an Outgoing person, you may find there are certain group situations where you feel uncomfortable. Even though you are usually talkative and expressive, if you're invited to a meeting where you don't know anyone, you may be quiet, even somewhat shy until you get to know the other people. Or, maybe you find yourself at a party where you're a stranger and a bit out of place, you may feel uneasy and actually come across as quiet and reserved. The difference for Outgoing persons like you is that once you do feel comfortable, you'll join in with conversations more readily than Reserved individuals. Even when comfortable, Reserved people will gravitate to one-on-one conversations and be less likely to join in on group interactions.

Not a measure of the need for alone time

Both Reserved and Outgoing people need time alone for different reasons and they need different amounts. Reserved individuals need to move away from people interactions and stimulation (music, conversation, talking, mingling, etc.) sooner and more frequently. Outgoing individuals can enjoy group interactions for longer, yet there still comes a point when they also need alone time to recharge. The amount of time needed for this recharging also varies. Outgoing individuals rebuild their energy more quickly and are ready to reengage sooner than Reserved individuals. For example, a quiet evening at home reading or engaging in a hobby might recharge an Outgoing individual. However, a Reserved person might need the entire weekend and still be thinking about how great an extra day or two of solitude might be.

Not the same reactions to stimuli

Reserved individuals are over stimulated by the environment, particularly intense interpersonal interactions. Outgoing people are under stimulated. This causes Reserved individuals to try to shut out the environment by "going inside," particularly when stressed. Outgoing people will do just the opposite. When stressed or bored they try to draw in the environment; turn up the music, connect with people, go to a gathering, etc. This engagement energizes them.

Summary Worksheet–Scale B, Responding

To create a quick, visible summary, identify your preference on this trait and check (√) the phrases that best describe your Work Style. Then, place an **X** next to the traits that fit your Personal Style.

Scale B: Responding

RESERVED: You respond to others in a quiet, reserved manner, and:

___ Are most at ease interacting with others one on one.

___ Keep your emotions rather private and self-contained.

___ Get energized when alone and away from activity.

___ Prefer to think problems through alone to clarify your feelings.

___ Use few gestures and facial expressions when you talk.

___ Contact friends and acquaintances occasionally.

OUTGOING: You respond to others in a talkative, expressive manner, and:

___ Interact easily with many people and groups.

___ Share emotions openly and freely.

___ Get energized by people contact and lots of activity.

___ Prefer to talk problems out with others to clarify feelings.

___ Use many gestures and expressions when talking.

___ Contact friends and acquaintances frequently.

Time and tide wait for no one.
—St. Marher

The strongest of warriors are these two—Time and Patience
—Leo Tolstoy

——*/ /*——

Chapter 7

Scale C: Pacing

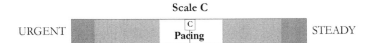

Scale C

URGENT | C | STEADY
Pacing

Scale C measures the speed and rhythm at which you make decisions and take action. The two opposite preferences are Urgent and Steady. Pacing involves both mental and physical activity and is used to describe such behaviors as your movement, speaking rate, and speed at making decisions. Think of this scale, Pacing, as the tempo at which you interact and engage with the world. Differences will become most apparent when two people make decisions at a different pace and they are working together on a team or are living together.

Locate your score on Scale C

Take a look at your results and identify whether you scored more toward the Urgent or Steady side of Scale C.

The left extreme, the Urgent preference, describes a tendency to make fast decisions, take action quickly, and physically move (i.e. walk and talk) at a rapid pace. The right side, the Steady preference, describes the tendency to take extended time when making decisions, move into action only after carefully considering options, and physically walk and talk with more deliberate, measured pace.

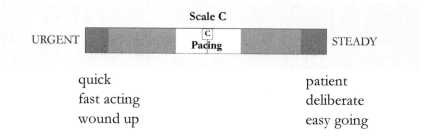

| | **Scale C** | |
| URGENT | [C] Pacing | STEADY |

quick	patient
fast acting	deliberate
wound up	easy going

URGENT

Descriptions of the URGENT Preference:

You consider a few important options before deciding.

You gather what you consider only the most important or relevant options, quickly sort out the pros and cons, and then make fast decisions. Selecting among the options you've deemed the most important allows you to move ahead and avoid getting bogged down with delays. You prefer action over non-action, and quick movement over slow movement.

You get things done by taking action quickly and making changes

Usually action and readiness for change accompany quick decision-making. If you scored Urgent you are probably good at moving from the decision-making phase to the action and implementation stage. You will tend not to second-guess, look back, or detour from your decisions. This helps you move forward and movement ahead is important to you.

Motor boat on turbo charge
People who work with Jim have nicknamed him the "motor boat." He speeds into situations, particularly problems, makes fast assessments of the things that need to be done, and takes action. Most of the time, team members are appreciative of the burst of energy and resolve to make things happen. Sometimes, particularly in areas where he has little experience, he goes the in wrong direction and makes matters worse with impulsive decisions. He always responds with a smile and says, "better to do something rather than nothing." There are times co-workers feel that this is true, but other times not so much.

You prefer short-term projects requiring quick responses.

You prefer work assignments where there are frequent changes and lots of variety. Often, these involve roles where you are included on several projects, ideally each somewhat short-term in nature, and require lots of quick decision-making. Start-up, rescue, and transition projects often have these characteristics. You thrive in these situations because they allow you to make good use of your preference for quickly considering a few key options, making fast decisions, and taking action. You'll also tend to enjoy job roles that include a wide variety of responsibilities with lots of new issues to deal with and fires to put out. These keep you from getting bored.

You work with a fast-paced, urgent style.

You typically move fast, talk quickly, and appear to be in a hurry. You are usually rushing from here to there, checking in, checking out, and switching from one project to another. The amount you accomplish depends on your competence. If you're skilled and experienced, you'll complete many tasks quickly and get a lot done. If you lack competence, you'll jump in on a lot of projects but may not want to get involved for the full duration, preferring instead to move on to other opportunities. You may create a lot of motion and activity, and this can disrupt some teams that are trying to focus on a key priority. Watch out that you don't leave a stack of projects started, but not quite finished.

You react quickly when frustrated and angered.

Because you react quickly, this may come across as either authentic honesty or critical impatience. If you notice someone doing something wrong, you may voice your disapproval in the form of a snappy remark or correction. Your frustration and impatience can cast a cloud on the situation and cause others to freeze up rather than jump into action like you really want. You may find that as an Urgent person, you tend to get angry quickly and react instantly, but you also cool off fast. If this is the case, you'll find it helpful to let others know when you've calmed down and the coast is clear.

Reaction times can be compared to the way fuses work with explosive devices. Urgent individuals have short, fast-burning fuses while Steady individuals have long, slow-burning ones. One upside to being Urgent is that when you get upset, others won't have to wait long before they learn about it. But, you'll need to be sure that your fast reactions aren't always negative ones. Learn to compliment and validate others just as quickly as you correct them. This will help others feel safe around your Urgent style and allow them to see the advantages of your action-oriented preference.

You make most decisions quickly—"Opportunity knocks once."

As an Urgent person, your preference for acting quickly helps you seize the moment when an opportunity arises. You're able to make fast decisions without waiting to gather more information or explore other alternatives. This helps you avoid missing opportunities, special deals, or product discounts that come infrequently.

However, sometimes you may make snap decisions that you later regret. You might purchase things you don't really need; loan money to someone who overpromises and under delivers; or mistakenly believe that some sales offerings are time limited when they really are not. However, chances are that instead of delaying things, you'd rather adjust to poor snap decisions than live with the regret of not having acted on opportunities. You'll have to accept that you'll make some impulsive mistakes along the way.

The judge and the jury.

His co-workers say that Paul has a kind heart and is one of the most well intended individuals they know. He's always willing to help. But when he meets someone new or gets involved with a project, he makes fast decisions and closes down options quickly. This decisiveness is particularly sharp when it comes to people. If he is suspicious of someone, he quickly decides they can't be trusted. If someone makes mistakes, he concludes they are incompetent. On the other hand, if he likes someone, he will just as quickly give that person the benefit of the doubt and extra chances to improve and not give it a second thought. Since these snap decisions come so quickly and are so irrevocable, he has been labeled, the one man "judge and jury."

Your strengths include:

Taking fast action when opportunities arise that require immediate decisions.

As an Urgent individual you'll excel at moving forward when action needs to be taken. You will speed ahead when an opportunity presents itself. You may even choose a career that immerses you in action such as emergency tech specialist, policeman, fireman, business entrepreneur, adventure sports promoter, etc. where your preference for making fast decisions and taking action are assets. Any career or profession can have roles that require quick problem solving and fast action and you'll gravitate to those positions.

Quickly eliminating options that seem to confuse an issue or delay action.

You have an innate ability to sort through options and alternatives and quickly make choices that lead to action. This helps you move decisions ahead. Your urgency helps you eliminate many peripheral or secondary issues that aren't helpful and helps you push teams forward. You'll tend to seize opportunities and be an early adopter.

How You Walk your Walk

You are probably known for your fast-paced, hurried manner. You:

- walk fast with snappy gestures
- have a quick rate of speech
- jump into projects quickly

How You Talk your Talk

Following are some samples of how you might say things and what you may be attending to:

- *Let's make a decision and get on with this.*

- *Okay, I'll start this project and work a little bit on the other task, and get several things under way.*
- *I can accomplish more by getting involved in a number of things.*

Motto:

- Speak now or forever hold your peace.
- It's now or never.
- The early bird gets the worm.

STEADY

Descriptions of the STEADY Preference:

You make decisions only after much deliberation and consider many options before deciding.

As a person with a Steady pace, you consider many choices and alternatives before making decisions and taking action. You like to be sure you have thoroughly explored all the possibilities and thought through many potential outcomes before making your final selections. When you've taken plenty of time, you feel more confident in your decisions.

You may also find yourself getting close to making a decision on something and then second guessing it and choosing to delay it until you have had time to explore various other possibilities. If you uncover new information, this can send you in an entirely different direction. This has certain payoffs such as discovering unknown options and new approaches; but, other people, particularly Urgent individuals, may feel you're taking too long and will push you to make a decision.

The consumer of Consumer Reports

Larry doesn't make any decision without thinking about it long and hard. Even something relatively inexpensive isn't purchased until the reviews and reports on it are studied and compared. This drives his employees crazy when they just want to get a purchase order and buy a new electronic device. He checks updates and postpones purchases until the next upgrade comes out or good reviews appear. "No need to be in a hurry." he says. He may miss special discounts and sales, but he seldom buys things that are mistakes.

You get things done by "sticking with it" and persisting.

You are very good at sticking with long drawn-out projects or tasks that require a lot of patience. This is particularly true when you have a high interest in the project and strong motivation to complete it. This doesn't mean that you necessarily like all jobs that take a long time, but it does mean that you can persist and adapt to such requirements and tend to do this better without experiencing the impatience and frustration that often surfaces with Urgent individuals.

You also tend to stick with interpersonal relationships. You tend to be loyal and weather the ups and downs of communication without reacting too quickly to issues that upset you. The positive side of this is that you typically have a number of "old" friendships and personal relationships. On the downside, you may maintain some draining or even unhealthy relationships beyond the point where others would have ended them.

You prefer long-term projects requiring calculated responses.

You function well in positions that make use of your patient and persistent style. When tasks take more time than expected, you tend to hang in there and stick with them. You have the capacity to buckle down for the long haul and not get frustrated and impulsively quit. You're also good at completing the time-consuming planning needed for long drawn out projects. This doesn't mean that you don't get bored if a job gets overly redundant; you just tend to be able to rise above the boredom and plod through the tasks instead of quitting.

The long, long range planner.
Mildred plans projects months, even years in advance. Team members usually appreciate this, but they get frustrated when Mildred is put in charge of new projects. She doesn't think in terms of weeks or months; she methodically considers how things will work out years from now. She always says, "patience and planning pays off."

However, for more urgent co-workers this can take away the excitement and thrill of new projects. They sometimes moan and groan when they're asked to run the numbers in different ways or review the budget one more time. But, they have learned it's quicker to comply and keep moving forward rather than question her thorough planning. Usually the projects she is involved with are very successful.

You work with an even-paced, consistent style.

You prefer to pace yourself at a fairly even cadence when completing projects. You may appear to be going at a smooth and steady rate even when internally you feel quite pressured and rushed. Others may not recognize when you're under stress because you don't tend to show it in typical ways. When you use your preferred Steady, deliberate, non-stressed groove, you can chip away at work tasks for long periods of time. You may even achieve more and produce better results at the end of the day than the "fast-slow-fast" cycling more Urgent individuals tend to use.

You react slowly when frustrated and angered.

You tend to be even-tempered and slow to react when you're upset. You're probably appreciated for your calm, placid style. You usually aren't ruffled by small things and even when upset, you may not show this outwardly. You tend to consider things with much thought, weighing the pros and cons, before you react. This doesn't mean you never blow up; it just indicates that when frustrated, your fuse burns long and slow before you eventually explode.

Volcanoes are known to erupt

If anyone could ignore small irritations, mistakes, and inconveniences it was Valerie. She was known for her easygoing, patient leadership style. However, upon rare occasions little things at the office would build up and then the smallest of incidents, something that she would normally ignore—like the proverbial straw that breaks the camel's back—would cause her to blow up. Then, erupt she would! Co-workers, even other managers, would run for cover. Sometimes, they would even warn each other that she had gone ballistic. Usually Valerie's explosions subsided quickly and she and her team members were able to laugh off the atypical behavior.

You make most decisions cautiously—"Timing is everything."

You like to take your time making decisions and carefully think through the pros and cons of each possible option. Underlying this is the belief that, given enough time and alternatives, the right choices will surface. Sometimes this is true, but other times it isn't. In either case, it creates the feeling that when the timing is right, everything will fall into place.

Restless nights.

Steve, a division head, always says he sleeps better knowing that a big decision hasn't yet been made and that he'll have time the next day to think it through some more. His department manager, Karen, is just the opposite. She is Urgent and says she sleeps better knowing a decision has been made and she can come in the next day and get to work. Steve, on the other hand, finds that leaving things open allows him more time to get comfortable with the direction he's leaning and not feel as if he has forgotten to consider certain items. When Steve and Karen are trying to make a decision that impacts both of their work areas, there are some restless nights and frustrating morning meetings either way.

Your strengths include:

Holding back on decisions until better opportunities have time to surface.

Delaying decision-making often provides time for other opportunities to surface that you may not otherwise have considered. Holding back on decisions works as a strength in complex situations where alternatives are slowly revealed and only surface with time and discussion. Your patience can provide a way to weave these alternatives into the discussions and final decisions.

Patiently staying open to alternatives that show promise and others may have closed their minds to.

It isn't always easy to stay open to more alternatives when there is pressure to make a decision. You have the wherewithal to hold space and time for more input and resist pressure-laden time schedules. It requires a lot of patience and persistence to remain open and undecided when others are racing, even pushing, to get decisions made. Sometimes you'll even face cultural values that imply that a fast pace and quick action is "good" and that taking time is "bad." This isn't always so, it's only a bias. Your Steady personality trait helps to even this out and allow for more consideration and time, particularly on important decisions.

How You Walk Your Walk

You tend to convey an easy-going style and:
- move about in a relaxed, unhurried manner
- appear calm and at ease, frequently even when upset
- use smooth, non-frantic gestures
- amble along rather than rush hectically
- converse and pick your words somewhat slowly
-

How You Talk Your Talk

Following are some samples of how you might say things and what you may be attending to:

- *Let's think about this awhile and not make any hasty decisions. The right decision will become clear with time.*
- *Let's hang in here and work away and complete everything, even if it takes all night.*
- *I can accomplish more if you give me time to focus on one task at a time and don't interrupt me too much.*

Mottos:

- Timing is everything.
- Take your time and do it right the first time.

What Scale C is NOT

Not a measure of productiveness

Steady and Urgent individuals can be equally productive. They can both produce good results, but they will accomplish these through different behavior patterns. Urgent people will rush in and do things quickly, perhaps sometimes skipping what they feel are some unnecessary steps. Steady individuals will take their time, do it more slowly, and usually complete most of the steps. If they are both committed and motivated, the results can be equally good, but the pathways will be different.

Not a measure of the amount of energy

Steady people may have as much or more energy than Urgent people, but they simply burn their energy at a different rate. Steady people might pace themselves and go along at a consistent level of energy burn all day long. In doing so, they may accomplish the same amount, if not more, than Urgent people who go at tasks fast and furiously, take breaks, go again fast and furiously, take other breaks, and generally follow a start/stop pattern. Work values and motivation provide a better measure of productivity and energy, rather than a person's score on Pacing.

Not a measure of the quality of decisions

The quality and outcome of decisions reflect knowledge, experience, judgment, intelligence, and a host of other factors. Consider two people who score Steady. Person A is experienced and knowledgeable and might take a long time deliberating an issue and end up making very intelligent decisions. Person B is also Steady, and may, like Person A take a long time deliberating options. However— perhaps due to lack of experience and knowledge—Person B makes a poor decision.

In a similar fashion, a knowledgeable Urgent person might make a "smart" decision quickly and a less experienced Urgent person might make a "dumb" decision equally as fast. Again, the quality of a decision is not related to the pace used in making the decision.

Not a measure of the "right" way to do things.

Effectiveness means doing the "right" things the "right" way and meeting important deadlines. Even though they work at a different pace and make decisions at a different rate, both Steady and Urgent individuals can use their pace of activity to be effective. Likewise, both can fail at accomplishing tasks, not because of their pace, but because of other factors.

Busy doesn't always produce results

Jack and Marian, both score Urgent on Scale C. They both work fast and appear to get a lot done because they are always in motion and appear to be very busy. Marian focuses on the most important priorities, jumps in, and finishes them. Jack appears equally busy, but he often gets distracted by less critical matters, jumps from project to project, gets distracted, and in the end, accomplishes few meaningful results. Since they are both Urgent, they both appear busy to an outside observer. However, Marian uses her urgency to get important things done first, while Jack uses his urgency so inefficiently that many of his frantic actions accomplish little.

Now consider two Steady individuals.

Steady and focused or Steady and unfocused

Steve, a motivated and efficient Steady individual, works persistently and deliberately on critical tasks and usually accomplishes a lot. He is a self-starter and when given an extended project, he hangs in there and works away until he is finished. Marty, who is also Steady, works equally tirelessly and persistently. He has a good work ethic. However, Marty frequently gets derailed and invests his time on less important things. Often, at the end of a long day has worked hard and long, but has accomplished little of value compared to Steve. Both are Steady, but they produce quite different results.

The real goal is to focus on doing the important things first, regardless of the pace you prefer. Also, your motivation to work hard and do a good job is more important than the Pacing you prefer to use. The objective is to make good decisions, regardless of how quickly or slowly you make them. Some decisions will require more research and deliberation because of their importance; others because of time issues require fast decisions. Urgent and Steady individuals can collaborate to even each other out.

Summary Worksheet–Scale C, Pacing

To create a quick, visible summary, identify your preference on this trait and check (✓) the phrases that best describe your Work Style. Then, place an **X** next to the traits that fit your Personal Style.

Scale C: Pacing

URGENT: You take action, make decisions quickly, and

____ Consider a few important options before deciding.

____ Get things done by taking action quickly.

____ Prefer short-term projects requiring quick responses.

____ Work with a fast-paced, urgent style.

____ React quickly when frustrated and angered.

____ Move ahead fast—"Opportunity knocks but once."

STEADY: You take action and make decisions after much deliberation and:

____ Consider many options and alternatives before deciding.

____ Get things done with persistence and patience.

____ Prefer long-term projects requiring calculated responses.

____ Work with an even-paced, consistent style.

____ React slowly when frustrated or angered.

____ Move ahead cautiously—"Timing is everything."

A place for everything, and everything in its place.
— Anonymous

One of the advantages of being disorderly is that one is constantly making exciting discoveries.
— A. A. Milne

—//—

Chapter 8

Scale D: Organizing

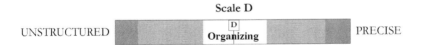

Scale D assesses your preference for structuring time, prioritizing tasks, and handling details. The two opposite extremes are Unstructured and Precise. If you score Unstructured, you are flexible, adaptable, and nonconforming. You like to "go with the flow" and tend to be resistant to systems and rules. If you score Precise, you attend closely to details, prefer set time schedules and procedures, and function best in orderly settings.

A quick phrase that sums this trait up is "piles vs. files." Unstructured people tolerate and work around piles; Precise people want things ordered and put away in files. Precise individuals order as a priority and often comment that they can't start to work in a disorganized or messy setting. Unstructured individuals work around the piles and organize after a project is finished. However, even once things are cleaned up and put in place, they don't stay that way very long for Unstructured people. Soon their system and order deteriorate. Precise individuals organize regularly and work to keep their systems in place.

Locate your score on Scale D

Take a look at your results and identify whether you scored more toward the Unstructured or Precise preference.

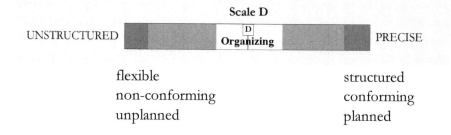

UNSTRUCTURED — flexible, non-conforming, unplanned — PRECISE — structured, conforming, planned

UNSTRUCTURED

Description of the UNSTRUCTURED preference:

You strive to have your time unstructured and plans flexible.

As an Unstructured person you are most comfortable having flexibility in your schedule and keeping your time relatively unplanned and free of tightly scheduled commitments. Although you can adapt to time clocks and meetings, you generally resist these systems because they feel restrictive and limiting.

You frequently see time as approximate. When you say you will get to something in a couple of minutes, you really mean you'll attempt to get to it as soon as possible. In contrast, when Precise individuals say they'll work on something in a couple of minutes, they are thinking of exactly 120 seconds. Misunderstandings arise when Unstructured and Structured individuals discuss time. For Precise people, time is black and white. For Unstructured individuals, it's shades of grey.

You tend to postpone organizing and attending to details.

You tend to put off organizing and attending to the many small details of work and personal life. You may let paperwork, bills, e-mail, texts, and the organizing of minor tasks pile up before jumping in and getting caught up. If important issues come up, such as an emergency request or a late notice on a bill, you'll get to it more quickly. However, in general you let the little issues, or what you consider to be unimportant things, accumulate and you invest your time elsewhere, particularly in creative projects.

What's next? Who knows?

Planning her complicated schedule is one of the most stressful things in Lauren's day. She would prefer to just go with the flow and see what priorities or emergencies come up. But, since there are so many time sensitive deadlines and various people depending on her, she has to flex and get very organized. She forces herself to accomplish this on a day-to-day basis, but it is challenging for her. Even when using calendars, phone notices, and messages she struggles to get everything done in a timely fashion. She looks forward to reaching a point in her career where she can have a more open, unstructured schedule.

You use unconventional procedures to accomplish tasks.

You're often very creative at coming up with unusual ways to accomplish tasks. You typically enjoy working on projects with no set guidelines or constraining rules where you're free to just figure out what will work and develop new procedures.

You are good at bringing diverse ideas together to create new ones because you do not get stuck on or restricted by old belief systems or ways of doing things. This makes it possible for you to approach projects with creative and unusual thinking. Because you naturally find rules and procedures limiting, you are willing to break existing ones and instead come up with an innovative, free-flowing approach.

Speakers on the edge

Dave and Jan are both exceptional speakers, but they approach training in completely different ways. Jan is Unstructured and every time she prepares a course, she tries something new. She considers outlines to be general guidelines. She adds a little of this and a dash of that until she has created a great session. However, don't ask Jan for notes; she seldom remembers exactly what she did or exactly what she presented. Dave, on the other hand, is Precise. He creates minute-by-minute outlines and then follows them exactly. When he does experiment, he keeps careful notes and can describe in detail the new material he presented. Some participants like attending Jan's session because they are spontaneous and fun. Others prefer Dave's structured courses and they keep his detailed workbooks for years.

You like to keep your plans open and somewhat unpredictable.

Settings and work environments that are very structured and predictable may tend to feel restrictive and limiting to you. You prefer to keep your schedule and plans flexible and manage priorities as they come up without having to schedule everything. You enjoy the unpredictable or unforeseen situations that surface and need to be resolved. You like the flexibility (there's that word again) of being able to drop everything and attend to these without conforming to a schedule.

Socially, you also enjoy keeping plans open and just seeing what opportunities and possibilities come up. Instead of having a weekend planned out in detail, you'd rather just meet friends at the last minute and see where the evening takes you. For you, adventure comes in the unfolding of events and unexpected possibilities that emerge.

No time for a time organizer

Sasha is Unstructured and to get better control of her busy schedule, she recently downloaded a time organizer for her cell phone. However, she hates to use it. She has tried other calendars before, however usually after a short period of time she quits entering data, it gets out of date, and eventually she forgets she even has it. For Sasha, time itself is rather ambiguous thing, not an exact science. If she tells someone she'll meet them at 6:00 PM she means anywhere from 5:30 to 6:30 PM. Her more organized co-workers want her to break this pattern and they send her new online calendars and scheduling apps to try. Chances are that if Sasha tries them, she will only use them for a limited time.

You proceed on projects before reading all the directions.

When detailed instructions come with new products, you rarely read through them. If a policy manual is provided for project management, you'll probably set it aside until you face a problem. Instead of reviewing and studying these ahead of time, you prefer to jump in and figure things out as you go. Then, only when you run into complications or get off track will you pull out the directions and guidelines.

Copy machine stand mishap

Kenny is in charge of technology for his organization and when a new computer, printer, or sound system arrives, he just sets the instructions aside and starts putting it together. He likes to be unstructured and do things without planning. Even when he gets off track, it is more enjoyable to experiment with various options, to try and fail, rather than read the directions. This doesn't carry over to mechanical skills. When he tried to assemble a shelving stand for a new copy machine without reading the directions it was a disaster. He had to start over—at his office manager's insistence—and lay out the parts carefully, count them, and get organized before trying again.

You take pride in doing things in new and different ways.

You enjoy trying new and different ways to do things even though systems, policies, and proven ways to succeed may already exist. Sometimes, this helps you discover new approaches, but other times this causes you to get needlessly derailed. If systems have been thoroughly researched, you would probably be better served to find ways to comply and learn how to do them efficiently. However, if there are no proven pathways, your unstructured strategies may help you uncover something that works even better.

You get frustrated by too many guidelines and rules.

Although you can comply with rules and guidelines, your personality tendencies lead you to find ways to work around them. Everything from submitting required reports, making bill payments by due dates, returning calls within certain times, or even checking text messages and e-mail can be irritating. You may find that you have to create elaborate reminder systems to keep these things ordered in your mind.

Your strengths include:

Discovering and following innovative ways to reach goals.

You're usually a great source of new ideas and creative strategies to projects. You can be quite good at applying your non-conforming style and flexibility to problems that require innovative approaches. You'll be willing to think of ideas that break conventional ways of doing things and perhaps bend the rules that have been followed too literally in the past.

Working around disorganization and getting work done in situations that might bother other people.

At times, you're able to focus on the work that needs to be done and ignore the immediate surroundings, even if they are somewhat disorganized. You can deal with situations as they are and not get overly distracted by details, "shoulds" and "should not's." This allows you to work around things and cope fairly well in settings that may be confusing or chaotic.

On a less important level, very Precise individuals, might look into your office, study, or personal space and think it looks disorganized and messy. Usually this doesn't bother you if you're busy meeting a deadline or focusing on something that needs to be done soon. You find ways to ignore the clutter. Your pattern is to complete projects first, and then clean up later. If you're really busy, it is probably easy to keep postponing the latter.

You tend to be big-picture oriented and fairly good at seeing the forest rather than the trees. This may lead you to look past small issues and focus on the bigger goals that you want to achieve.

How you walk your walk

You:

- arrange your desk by piles, rather than files
- say, "Don't touch a thing, I know right where everything is."
- let your work area get very messy before cleaning it up
- allow your closet to become jumbled and "creatively" organized.
- clean up in binges, rather than keeping things organized.
- prefer casual or non-traditional clothing.

How you talk your talk

Following are some samples of how you might say things and what you may be attending to:

- *Here's the report. I haven't worked out all the bugs, but it gives the big picture. We can deal with the details later.*
- *There need to be fewer rules and regulations around this company. Our best ideas are tied up with all the red tape, policies, and procedures.*
- *If you want me to do something, just turn it over to me and let me figure it out. Don't look over my shoulder or require me to do it your way.*

Mottos:

- Rules were made to be broken.
- You and I travel to the beat of a different drum.

PRECISE

Descriptions of the Precise preference:

As a Precise structured individual, you like order and seek to have things planned and systems in place. You organize projects and events ahead of time and this helps you get things done effectively and efficiently. You probably keep a calendar in place and your workspace is likely neat and organized; you might even keep your desk cleared of everything except the requirements of the task at hand.

> ### A storage room of order
> Michelle is super organized. She keeps lists of her lists. Her office cubical is meticulously set up for efficiency. She considers herself a closet queen. At home she hangs all her shirts on the same types of hangers, facing in the same direction, sorted by color. Her slacks are folded and stacked much like a clothing store display. Shoes are lined up and placed together by season. So when Michelle gets time to organize the office storage room she imposes a similar order. Paper clips go here, letterhead there, mailing envelops all facing to the left, etc. Michelle says this helps her accomplish things more quickly because she loses no time looking for things. However, she sure gets frustrated when co-workers mess up her system.

You tend to organize details in a timely and thorough fashion.

You create systems and procedures that maintain order and ensure effectiveness. You put things in their place and keep them there because that brings efficiency and predictability to your world. This can spill over to your work and personal world in various ways.

At work, depending on your roles and responsibilities, the systems you create could range all the way from complex product development strategies and operational procedures down to basic filing systems. In either case, you'll approach them by putting a system in place. Your underlying mission is to use order to "achieve success and reduce stress."

At home in your personal life, you'll tend to carefully structure most of your activities, whether it be exercise time, household cleaning, errands, or how you organize the spices in your food cabinet. You'll seek to have things in a specific order and you'll try to keep things that way.

> **A vacation well planned**
> Stephen is known for creating plans and working those plans. He constructs detailed lists that track all the steps necessary for completing projects. It's no small wonder that he is a highly successful project manager. He carries this same diligence over to his home life and he plans family vacations down to the hour. He knows just where his family will be each day, where they will be lodging, and even the best restaurants in the area. This reduces his stress; but doesn't always fit for his unstructured family members. They often want to do things more spontaneously and just figure things out as they go. That's not for Stephen, he says that would make him too nervous and he'd actually have less fun and want to go back to work.

You use established procedures to accomplish tasks.

When working on projects and completing tasks, you prefer following established rules and procedures. If a procedure has been worked out to accomplish some task and it has been proven to work, you see little reason to deviate from it or make any changes. You'll probably be concerned that even small alterations—the types of things others might not notice—could dramatically impact the process and flow of things, the type of issues you notice. If anything, the fact that the procedure currently works is convincing evidence that it should be followed and not changed for the sake change. You generally adhere to the philosophy, "If it isn't broken, don't fix it."

You like plans clearly set and somewhat predictable.

You prefer to have your work and activities scheduled and planned. While you can adapt to last-minute schedule changes, you often find these frustrating and a bit stressful. You like to "plan your work" and "work your plan." Continuous changes in schedules, without input into how to control these in the future, can become quite frustrating. In your mind, schedules exist for a reason: to avoid delays and problems.

Timeliness is an important concept to you. Not only should details be taken care of; they should be attended to promptly, even ahead of schedule. This helps avoid any problems or delays that might come up. You seek to get such things as memos written, bills paid, and correspondence done on time. In your personal life, you usually get such things as your trip packing and your holiday shopping done early. You keep track of birthdays and anniversaries and have systems in place that help remind you to get notes and messages sent out on time.

Nothing to chance

Danielle is a stickler for timeliness. She plans her schedule carefully and checks it frequently. She enters extra time for getting from one place to another, such as walking to a different building or even making it down long hallways. She does this to ensure that she arrives at meetings on time, or preferably early. She leaves nothing to chance when it comes to scheduled appointments. She often wishes co-workers would do the same, but understands that they operate differently. She wonders at times if she is too compulsive about time.

You proceed on projects only after reading all the directions.

You see the reason for directions, manuals, and instructions; they help you get things "right." You have a difficult time imagining doing anything without a good manual or set of directions. These guides are designed to make completing tasks easier and prevent mistakes. Not only do you read these manuals, you read through them in a sequenced order, from the first page to the last. (If Unstructured individuals have even kept their manuals, they probably just skip over certain chapters and read only what interests them at that moment.)

The only exception to this comes when the manuals and directions are poorly written. If you spot typos, errors in identifying parts, or omissions, you'll most likely get irritated. Nothing is more infuriating than poorly designed instructions. That is because you believe they should be followed step-by-step and you can't do this if they are difficult to understand?

You take pride in doing things in established, proven ways.

You are adept at creating systems and procedures. Once you find ways to do things in ways or sequences that work efficiently you will follow these and encourage others to do the same. You're likely a repository of proven strategies and methods. Plus, you probably keep these techniques on file in an orderly fashion where you can readily access them when you or others need help.

How to use a proven "how to."

Maria is often faced with implementing the decisions of others. Since she prides herself on seldom making mistakes, she reads all directions, carefully follows the guidelines, and even searches for and watches "how to" videos before proceeding on projects. That's what the instructions are for," she says. Frequently she even follows up by making her own instructional videos. Since she is usually over prepared, she gets things done almost perfectly the first time around. She sees this as a strength and often wonders how others can just jump into projects without preparing first. She tries to lead by example and has found that this frequently rubs off on others.

You get frustrated by ambiguity and lack of specific guidelines.

You want clear and specific instructions for doing things. This comes from your drive to do things right and do them correctly the first time if at all possible. If clear instructions are not provided, you may worry that you might not be able to do the project correctly. When this occurs, you'll feel it could have been avoided if there had been better guidelines, manuals, and directions.

If you're delegating tasks to others, you're probably very good at providing lots of details and instructions. Precise co-workers usually appreciate this. Unstructured individuals however, may feel the detailed guidelines restrain them, sometimes to the point where they come to believe that you doubt their capability.

When projects are delegated to you, you prefer leaders to:
1) Write it out and give you a copy.
2) Go over these instructions in detail.
3) Allow you to ask questions to insure you have it right.
4) Give you a way to check in if problems arise.

Your strengths include:

Bringing order and structure to disorganized situations.

You can move into disorganized environments and quickly (if given permission or authority) bring order to chaos. You're able to see where systems have broken down and procedures have not been followed. You can almost instantly spot how a better way of doing things such as implementing a more efficient organizational system or setting up a structure that would improve things. Not only can you see these, you're probably skilled at helping others and put them in place. Devising methods for eliminating disorder, clutter, and unnecessary steps is part of the way you think.

Seeing ways to improve systems and policies that help projects flow smoothly.

Identifying ways to improve procedures and processes requires a different form of creativity. Usually "creativity" is used to describe unusual ways of doing things. But when applied to work flow, creativity involves the capacity to think of new, better ways of accomplishing goals. It demands that you devise improved procedures and envision the smallest of steps. Your creativity comes out in the ability to implement new ways to make projects flow smoothly. That's why you'll want to have some control of this process, otherwise, you'll get frustrated if you cannot implement the improved systems that you develop.

How you walk your walk

Whether it is your desk, room, or even automobile, you:
- organize your space meticulously
- keep most things filed or stored away
- dislike disorganization
- clean up your work area before starting on projects

How you talk your talk

Following are some samples of how you might say things and what you might be attending to:
- *Let me double check that report. It's easy to miss little typos or errors.*
- *Okay, I'm going to put that on this blue list, attached to the red list.*
- *Too many people in this organization just aren't following the rules and it creates chaos. We need a system that helps people comply better.*

Mottos:
- Rules were made to be followed, not broken.

- If you want it done right, you'd better do it yourself.
- Do it right the first time.
- If it isn't broken, don't fix it.

What Scale D Is Not

Not a measure of quality.

Both Unstructured and Precise individuals can produce high-quality work. Scale D measures a preference for the way people like to organize and manage the details of projects, not the final outcomes. Unstructured individual's desks may be piled with files, yet if they are experienced and smart, they may produce work of excellent quality. Precise individuals could maintain meticulously clean and organized work spaces, but if they are inexperienced and not motivated, they could produce poor quality results. The preference for orderliness does not produce quality. Intelligence, experience, and motivation are better predictors of quality than personality preferences.

Not a measure of creativity.

Unstructured individuals often approach projects from novel and unconventional angles. This does not mean these individuals are more creative than Precise people. Individuals who are Precise are often creative in envisioning new systems and processes that bring order and efficiency to work and home. In other words, they are creative in different ways. Each type of creativity has value.

Not a measure of ability to organize.

Many Unstructured individuals can be great organizers. They know how to put systems in place and can carefully track details. They may even value orderliness and predictability. Some have jobs requiring a lot of planning and order and they can succeed at these. However, they have to consciously work at this. Organizing comes more naturally to people with Precise personality preferences. So when Unstructured individuals take on these tasks, they have to move out of their comfort zone. They can develop the skill needed to do this and perform at high levels. However, these Unstructured individuals often say that they drop all this order and structure when they are at home and it is not required.

Whose car is this?

Angela is known as a brilliant surgeon who does everything by the book. She follows procedures carefully, maintains an immaculate operating room, and attends to every detail. She's constantly checking and double-checking everything. In her personal world however, Angela drops all of this structure and detail. Her car is a disaster zone. It is filled with fast food wrappers and all kinds of clutter. She says that she's naturally unstructured so when it doesn't matter to anyone, she doesn't attend to details. When health and lives are at stake however, she switches over and becomes compulsively detailed and precise.

Frequently, Unstructured individuals who work well together create special agreements. These include what tasks or areas will be organized, who does it, and other such arrangements.

Office peace solution

In their shared office, Karen and Joseph both value having a clean, organized workspace. However, both are Unstructured. They each have a pattern of creating piles and clutter. While their own piles do not bother them, the other person's piles do. They believe the smartest thing they ever did as co-workers was to have agreed to hire Lucy, a very precise and structured assistant, organizes files and puts things away using a meticulous color-coded system. Joseph and Karen laugh and say they achieve success because of Lucy.

Summary Worksheet—Scale D, Organizing

To create a quick, visible summary, identify your preference on this trait and check (√) the phrases that best describe your Work Style. Then, place an **X** next to the traits that fit your Personal Style.

Scale D: Organizing

UNSTRUCTURED: You strive to keep time unstructured and plans flexible, and:

__ Tend to postpone organizing and attending to details.

__ Use unconventional procedures to accomplish tasks.

__ Like plans open and somewhat unpredictable.

__ Proceed on projects before reading all the directions.

__ Take pride in doing things in new and different ways.

__ Get frustrated with too many guidelines and rules.

PRECISE: You strive to have your time structured, plans defined, and:

__ Tend to organize details in a timely and thorough fashion.

__ Use established procedures to accomplish tasks.

__ Like plans clearly set and somewhat predictable.

__ Proceed on projects only after reading all the directions.

__ Take pride in doing things in established, proven ways.

__ Get frustrated by ambiguity or lack of specific guidelines.

LEAD with INSIGHT

The whole is greater than the sum of its parts.
—Aristotle

I want freedom for the full expression of my personality.
—Mahatma Gandhi

—//—

Chapter 9

Considering Profile Shapes

Let's do the math. There are four traits measured by the *INSIGHT Inventory* and a range of 40 points on each trait. That means there are 40 times 39 times 38 times 37 and so on down to 1, for a total count of over 2 million possible combinations. That just takes into consideration one environment. Work Style. Add the other two million combinations for Personal Style and the number of possibilities become difficult to grasp. This means that there really is only one you. You are indeed as unique as your fingerprint.

Your profile shape, three lines connecting your scores on the four traits, provides a quick graphic of your personality preferences. Your profile shape makes it easy for you and others to visualize how you tend to behave. You can quickly see your most extreme tendencies and the differences in intensity from one scale to another. When comparing your Work Style and Personal Style results, the profiles make it possible to instantly spot similarities and differences.

Other people will notice your more extreme traits first and describe you in those terms. However, you are defined by the interactions of all four traits, as well as the influences from whichever environment you might be in. This can get complex so to simplify, it could be said that your personality profiles provide a way for you to see how your traits combine with each other and are adapted to a particular setting.

Extremes become descriptors

The farther from the center one of your scores plots, the more others will notice the characteristics descriptive of that score and see you in those terms. When others "blink" and sum you up as people do, they will focus on one or two of your most extreme traits. This is based on the tendency of people to simplify their descriptions of others to make communication short and crisp. We do it with many things, for example, physical traits. People have many physical attributes, but if we point someone out in a crowd, we would probably just describe a person with a few basic characteristics. "She's the tall woman wearing glasses." or "He's the elderly red-headed guy with the cap." Brief descriptions move conversations ahead easily.

Likewise, when describing the personality characteristics of others, people tend to use an abbreviated shortcut language. "He's very strong-willed and impatient." She's very tactful, but a stickler for the details and getting things done right." Describing a person with one or two extreme personality traits conveys just enough information to make a point. This pattern over simplifies others; yet most people do it. Learn which of your traits others will likely use to describe you. Generally speaking, you can look at one or two of your most extreme scores and assume that these will be the traits others notice.

On the other hand, when you have the opportunity to describe yourself to others, you'll want to expand and broaden the number of traits that you weave into the conversation. For example, you might say that at Work you are very Direct when presenting your point of view, fairly Reserved in groups, fast and Urgent to act on opportunities, and slightly structured and Precise when organizing your plan of action. This credits the influence of each trait and combines them in a way that gives others a quick overview of your personality strengths. Offering a broader description also gives others more points of conversation they can inquire about. This is particularly important in job interviews, career transition discussions, and new relationships.

Effects of trait interaction

Profile shapes are important because they combine the four independent traits. It's easy to think of each preference as functioning in isolation, but all four traits are constantly working together and layering their characteristics over the top of each other. Just as the colors of the fingerprint on the cover of this book, the combination of traits is what makes you the unique person you are. The following examples help demonstrate this.

Example: Terry

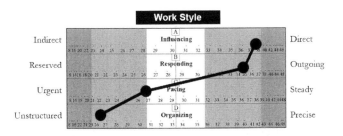

Terry scored Direct on scale A, Outgoing on Scale B, Urgent on Scale C, and Unstructured on Scale D. People describe him as candid and straightforward (Direct), friendly (Outgoing), quick to act (Urgent), and open to trying new things and breaking the rules (Unstructured). All four traits work together and form his overall style. However, it's likely other people will focus primarily on how assertive and decisive he is and just say something like, "Terry is strong-willed and quick to decide."

Profile changes in different environments

When you're discussing your personality profile with others, it's helpful to identify the environment in which you are describing your behavior. In the previous example, Terry may be different in his home setting and if so, sharing the changes he make will help others see more of him and better understand his behavior at work.

Profiles describe behavior tendencies not values

Personality trait preferences are different from core values. Values drive why a person gets involved with certain projects or efforts. Personality behaviors reveal how people walk and talk and interact when dealing with others.

The preacher and the pusher

Preacher   Pusher

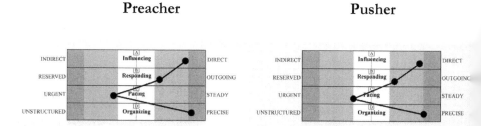

Consider two people with the same personality profile. One is a successful minister (the preacher) while the other is a corrupt drug dealer (the pusher). The preacher uses his Direct, Outgoing, Urgent, and Precise personality strengths to grow a ministry, perhaps founding a new church and serving with his candor, friendliness, fast action, and strong organizing skills.

The other person, the "pusher," uses the same Direct, Outgoing, Urgent and Precise strengths to manipulate and derive personal gain from the victimization of others. His frank direct style can be confused with straight-talk and truthfulness and his outgoing friendliness with genuine friendship. But, his focus is personal self-gain and he is indifferent to the wellbeing of others.

This example is meant to further indicate how personality profiles describe behavior and tendencies, not values and intentions. The lives that people live and the greater purposes they strive toward are determined by their values. Some people seek to serve others and be a force for good at work, within their families, and among their communities. Others choose self-serving paths of dishonesty, deception, and crime. Values predict life goals; personality preferences describe behavior.

Labeling

The *INSIGHT Inventory* avoids stereotyping different trait profiles. Labels, based on personality shapes, such as "manager," "entrepreneur," "salesman," "counselor," "specialist," and "workhorse," are not used because these often mix behavior with career interests and values. Labels can also cause problems when people mistakenly believe that a certain profile may be more successful in a certain job. If a person gets a profile that labels him as a "salesman" and he is functioning as a department supervisor, his manager might think that there is a poor person-job match.

The reality is that any person, when properly trained in the required technical skills, can succeed in about any job2 if the person is intelligent, motivated, and knows how to flex their personality style appropriately. If they are rigid and unmotivated, even what appears to be a good match will result in failure. Past behavior best predicts future performance. Job success cannot be predicted on personality preference profiles alone.

In summary:
- You are not one singular trait, but a combination of all four trait preferences interacting together.

- How you behave in different environments depends on the interplay between your traits and the pressures and opportunities within those environments.

- Once you know how to adapt to various environments and how your traits build on each other, you can use them to more effectively express your true self and unleash your personality strengths.

It is not the situation that makes the man, but the man who makes the situation.
— Fredrick William Robinson

—//—

Chapter 10

Investigating Profile Differences

You may behave differently in different settings. Sometimes changes are small, almost unnoticeable to anyone but you. At other times they may be rather noticeable to everyone. You may almost appear to have a different personality. The next step in this journey of self-discovery involves identifying the influences that various environments have on your behavior. As you become more aware of these influences, it will become easier to discover your "true you" and then move back to your strengths zone.

One strategy for adapting to certain environments is to bend a bit to adjust to any special demands, but never break away from your strengths. Flex your strengths, but try not to move too far away from them and for sure, don't lose sight of them. Another strategy is to develop the skill at behaving a certain way and practice this until you are really good and it comes almost naturally to you. In a way, you develop the ability or capacity to behave differently and it becomes an additional component of your leadership skill set. You become a person that bends when necessary with the ability to spring back to your innate self.

Behavior can change from one setting to another

If you've ever taken a personality assessment, reviewed your results, and thought, "But I'm not that way all the time!" Then you have identified one key problem with many assessments. Most do not take into consideration the strong influence that the environment has on behavior.

The *INSIGHT Inventory* is different. It factors in the pressures and stressors of two different environments, Work and Personal. It then helps you identify how your behavior may change as you move between these two settings. This takes you out of the box, away from generalized global descriptions, and helps you consider the impact of environmental pressures on your behavior.

Example: Steve adapting for career demands

Steve, a professional speaker, scores very Outgoing on his Work Style, but is Reserved at home in his Personal Style. Steve says that he sees himself as a relatively quiet person, even shy at times. However, when on stage, he takes on a different set of behaviors and becomes very talkative, animated, and quite the entertainer. He says that this shift does take a toll at times. After several speaking engagements in a row, he becomes stressed out and rather exhausted. When he gets home from these extended trips, he doesn't feel like interacting much with his family. He'll give everyone a hug and retire to a quiet place to read and be alone. He describes himself at those times as being "talked out" and needing time to recharge.

Steve says that there are other speakers with whom he works who are very Outgoing. Instead of being tired at the end of the week like he is; they are actually charged up. They are so Outgoing that they get energized the more sessions they book rather than drained. Steve is very talented and has learned the skills needed to hold and entertain an audience. He enjoys adapting his style and being Outgoing for a while, just as long as he does so in moderation. Then he looks forward to getting back to his Reserved, more natural style.

People see you as your behavior

While you will know when you're adapting your behavior in response to a given situation, other people may not realize it. Their perceptions are based on the behavior they see, not on characteristics or traits you may be flexing. In the example above, Steve may come across as very outgoing to most of his seminar participants. They probably enjoy his energy and enthusiasm and may find it difficult to believe that in a different setting, he is quite reserved and quiet.

If a group decides to join up and go out for dinner after the seminar, they might be surprised when Steve passes and says he needs some quiet time. It will seem out of character to them. However, to Steve the full day of being animated, humorous, and expressive is the out of character state.

This example may encourage you to think about the shifts you make, sometimes on a daily basis. The goal is to learn where your strengths zone is and how to flex when needed. Rarely does a perfect work world exist where you get to be completely yourself all the time. But, it is a nice objective to aspire to.

Also watch how you read others. Be conscious that as you develop your perceptions of people, you must take into consideration the setting or environment they are in and how it may be impacting them. The beauty of close friendships and family relationships is that you learn where the "true" person comes out and you accept this as okay. That's what friends are for. It's also good to extend this open attitude to your work colleges and accept that there may be dimensions to their personality that you don't see at work. They are more than their obvious behavior, as are you.

Behavior in two primary environments

Your *INSIGHT Inventory* profiles help reveal your behavior in two environments, Work and Personal. These are two settings where you spend much of your time. Most people make some adjustments between these two environments, perhaps on one or two traits. Typically, these are minimal and can be easily explained and understood by others. However, sometimes the shifts are quite extreme and point to some adaptions—often stressful—that you are making.

As you look at your results, allow time to really think through why you may shift from one setting to another on a particular trait. Congratulate yourself if it's a conscious shift, one you've developed skill at executing. But, if it is stress related, try to uncover some of the reasons and identify a pathway for getting back to your true strengths.

Some people make almost no change as they move from one setting to another. They might say, "What you see is what you get." Other people may change a great deal on all the four traits, and change noticeably. They are like chameleons. They completely adapt to their environment.

If your Work Style and Personal Style profiles are different, ask yourself if the changes are:
- intentional based on skill you have developed?
- stressful to make and energy consuming?
- easy to do and an enjoyable change of pace?

Your responses to these questions will help you identify reasons you may be flexing your traits between environments.

Expanding to other situations

Your Work Style and Personal Style profiles serve as a starting point to a broadening exploration of the various ways your behavior may change from one setting to another. You will find yourself in a variety of settings during your career, community involvement, and personal life. Once you've identified the similarities and differences between the broad areas of your work and personal worlds, you can start to investigate changes you may make in more specific settings, i.e. special project groups, when around a particular person, attending a sporting event, being at a family holiday with certain relatives, driving a car during rush-hour traffic, etc.

As you get skilled at identifying the environmental influences that bring out your strengths, you'll be better able to capitalize on them and stay at your best. You'll also get better at spotting the stressors that cause you to move out of your strengths zone. This will help you minimize your exposure to these or improve your skill at coping with them.

Nan adapting to home life

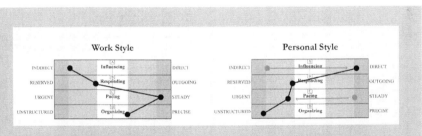

Nan, a mother of two teenagers says that she is Indirect and relatively Steady. Her job in a large company as a customer service agent actually draws upon these characteristics and this works. She once received an award for service.

At home, she struggles with controlling her teenagers who are going through some difficult times. As a result, she has been flexing her personal style to be much more Direct and Urgent. Nan purposely makes these shifts to enforce the rules of her home and control her strong-willed teenagers.

Nan says that flexing her behavior at home is stressful and at times very difficult. However, this firmer parenting style is working. She looks forward to the time when her children move on to jobs or college. She feels she could then shift back to a more easygoing, Indirect style and enjoy a more relaxed Steady pace of activity.

The "true" you

It might be clear which of your two profiles, describes you most of the time. You may take a quick look at your Work and Personal charts and know immediately which one is generally the better fit and best describes your strengths. Perhaps it is clear which profile reflects adaptations that you are making.

There is the possibility that you may have been making certain shifts for so long that they have become a part of who you are. This may invoke the image of a tree that has grown so long in a windy place that it has become tilted to one side. Its natural instinct is to grow upright, but years of adapting have caused it to take on an entirely different shape and grow sideways. If this has happened to you, the good news is that you've now identified this pattern and can begin to take steps for going back and rediscovering your "true" you and begin growing a different direction. This will be an exciting journey.

Another possibility for different Work and Personal profile shapes is that you're simply different in different settings. That's fine also. Talent at reading environmental expectations and pressures is a good thing. At least it can be as long as you know and any changes you make are intentional. However, if you're constantly flexing to please others and you've lost track of who you truly are, then it's time to pause. Rethink your what your personality trait preferences really are and identify when you're at your best. Then create a plan for getting there more often and staying there longer periods of time. That's a big step in rediscovering the real you.

Which environment reveals the most?

You may assume that your Personal Style would be the most descriptive of you, because at home you are perhaps more relaxed, at ease, and supposedly free to be your true self. This is true for many people, but this may not apply to you. Some people find that they experience more stress at home than you do at work. This could be true for you. Perhaps you are parenting small children or dealing with rebellious teenagers, or coping with a difficult family member. In such instances you may adapt your behavior more in your personal world than you do at work. In that case your "true" personality may show up more at work.

One way to try to identify how and why you may shift your behavior from one environment to another is to try and observe your behavior patterns from a distance. It's sometimes called a "view from 50,000 feet."

Here's how it works. Jump back to the example of Steve. If you were hovering in a satellite at a high altitude you might be able to see that he is most frequently Reserved and only Outgoing when presenting in front of groups. If you switched and observed Nan, the woman in the second example, you could see that she is soft-spoken and Indirect most of the time and only Direct and forceful when dealing with challenges from her teenagers. From a distance you would see the relative frequency of one behavior over another. However, if you were in Steve or Nan's shoes the immediacy of the behavior shift and the intensity might cloud your perception.

Therefore, try looking at your own behavior from a distance. This may help you see yourself from a different perspective and guide you in developing a clear image of what your true personality strengths are.

Why consider the setting and the pressures?

Your *INSIGHT Inventory* profiles also help you explore the range of your behavior. You may move only a small bit on Trait A from one environment to another. Others may barely notice the change. Or, you may make large shifts that everyone sees. As you develop better and better people skills, one goal is to learn to increase your range so you can flex and deal with a wider variety of people. However as you develop this extended range, you'll also need to increase your ability to snap back to your natural strengths zone. You want to be in charge of this skill. When you are, your relationships will begin to transform in positive ways. You'll find that you quit wishing others would change and instead you'll be the one who initiates change first. You'll flex to be who you need to be with them that will change the relationship.

The *INSIGHT Inventory* helps identify your strengths zone

Providing two profiles and creating this discussion of how you behave differently in different environments stands in sharp contrast to assessments that narrowly define your personality. The *INSIGHT Inventory*'s roots are in two social-psychological concepts: field theory and force field analysis. These models of explaining behavior were developed by Dr. Kurt Lewin in the 1940's at the University of Iowa and then further expanded when he was at the Center for the Study of Group Dynamics at MIT. Lewin believed that the pressures and opportunities in different environments could dramatically influence a person's behavior and needed to be taken into consideration alongside personality traits.

Many traditional personality assessments attempt to predict behavior by narrowing their descriptions of personality to primary factors or core traits. Others try to identify trait descriptors that support a particular creator's theory of types or traits. The *INSIGHT Inventory* strives instead to expand the understanding of behavior to include the influences of the surrounding environment and force fields.

Kurt Lewin, the father of modern social psychology, focused his studies on how people act in groups and situations, rather than how individuals act alone. Lewin grew up Jewish in a mixed neighborhood in Germany and had to flee with his family once the Nazi political military regime took power. He noted that neighbors who had been generous and befriended his family previous to the rise of Nazism were the same people who, in this new environment of fear, turned against his family. Lewin realized that they did not just wake up one day and decide to arbitrarily change their attitudes and behavior. Instead, the social political environment they were in and the consequences of certain actions caused them to change their behavior.

Later, as a pre-eminent social scientist, this influenced his conviction that behavior could not be separated from the environment from which it is contained. This led to his interest and life-long study of group dynamics and sociology; these led ultimately to the development of Field Theory.

Field Theory

Lewin was particularly interested in how individuals behave in groups. He believed small and large group behavior—rather than just individual behavior-that most impacted the world. Behavior within a family impacts all members; behavior within work teams impact the organization. He originated what is known as "field theory," the theoretical model maintaining that behavior is a function of one's personality within an environment.

Field theory is built on a short but revealing formula that explains why people behave the way they do:

$$B = f(P \times E)$$

Behavior is a function of the **P**ersonality within an **E**nvironment.

Change the pressures, expectations, and influences in the environment and typically people's behavior changes, regardless of their personality preferences. In his advanced work, Lewin created complex mathematical equations that put algebraic weight on the various pressures and opportunities within an environment. He developed elaborate formulas for predicting behavior while crediting these forces.

Lewin dramatically influenced the field of psychology and social psychology with the field theory model. While field theory explains "how" your behavior changes with various situations, it doesn't identify what factors cause it to change. For this, he developed what he called force field analysis.

Linda adapting to work requirements

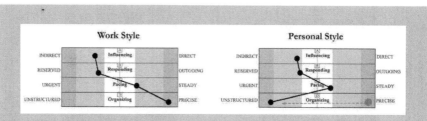

Linda, an accountant, scores very extreme Precise on Scale D: Organizing. This Precise Work Style has been a good fit for her because as an accountant she works in a very exacting way with numbers, data, and systems. She says that she enjoys doing this type of work, but that her natural style is really to be more Unstructured and that on her Personal Style profile, her score on Scale D actually falls quite far to the Unstructured side.

Linda feels that the change at work is a not a difficult one for her to make. In fact, she rather enjoys going in during the day and being very detailed and meticulous in her projects and records. At home, however, she says she doesn't even balance her own checkbook. She adds that the only time she feels that adapting is stressful is when year-end budget time rolls around and she has to rush through a lot of detailed work at the office in order to meet her final deadlines. Linda's preferred Pacing Style on Scale C is Steady. So the deadlines and pressures of ever changing project due dates are what stress her.

Force field analysis

In Lewin's theory, a force field is a composite of all the influences within an environment. The "environment" includes both external and internal force fields. External force fields consist of the settings you're in and the people you're around. This category includes things external to you such as the setting you are in, the groups and teams you are a part of, business cultures, family members, etc. Internal force fields include the expectations, pressures, and opportunities that exist within your mind. The internal force field also includes self-talk, the messages you give yourself, reactive patterns, conscious thoughts, memories, "should" and "should nots," etc.

The force fields in your work or school environments might include deadlines, rules, pressures, roles, stress, the needs of co-workers, superiors, and teachers are all pushing in on you and affecting your personality. Forces and pressures in your personal environment include family members, needs of friends, home care, finances, and so on. These force fields either encourage or inhibit certain behaviors. As you develop insight into yourself, you'll learn to identify the impact of all these various environmental pressures on your behavior.

The forces in your life

Some of the forces that end up impacting you are positive (encouragers) and some are negative (inhibitors). Keep in mind, other people may experience these same influences differently than you do. For one person, an unknown restaurant along a dark street is a positive experience because that person loves adventure and novelty. Another person, in the same situation, might see it as threatening because that person is fearful of new and unknown situations and is not a risk taker.

Who will speak?

Kendra is Outgoing and Vanessa is Reserved. When a meeting is held, individuals often need to speak spontaneously. Kendra enjoys this and jumps in and sharing stories about recent projects. Vanessa, on the other hand, experiences speaking as quite stressful. She is an excellent speaker, but she worries about being called and always feels it is out of her comfort zone. Vanessa would much rather listen to others and remain quiet. For Kendra, speaking is exciting and fits her Outgoing style but, for Vanessa who is Reserved, it's challenging.

Why do these theories matter?

The field theory foundation makes it possible for you to say, "I'm not this way all the time." It gives you an opportunity to explore how and why you change in different environments. Once you become aware of the impact of various influences, you can develop skill at changing your behavior in a specific setting to improve communication and relationships. It provides a gateway to change rather than a closed door defining you.

Boundaries, shells, and membranes

The work of Carl Jung, often labeled Jungian Theory, contends that there is a membrane or "shell" around each of us that helps us differentiate our "self" from others and the external world. Depending on how thick your shell is, your environment might affect your behavior a great deal, or not at all. Some people have a rather thick shell and aren't influenced much by their environment. They retain a strong sense of self at all times and don't easily change based on the environmental pressures. They may say something like, "What you see is what you get." They use this catchy phrase to say that they are generally the same in most situations.

Other individuals might have thin shells. They continually monitor their environment and adapt to the pressures, stresses, and personalities they experience. This adaptation can be helpful for pleasing others and avoiding conflict. However, thin shelled, quick-adapters might find that they have a tendency to lose their sense of self at times, a feeling of trying to be everything to everyone.

Adapting

Adapting is consciously adjusting your behavior to a broad environment for a long period of time. Flexing is adjusting your behavior temporarily to communicate better with another person. An important goal is to identify your strengths, own them, and then develop the ability to flex easily and also monitor how long you adapt to certain environments.

You might find that your goal is to thicken the membrane between self and environment so that you can be yourself more of the time. The goal for other people may be to soften the membrane so they can be more conscious of the needs of others and more adaptable. In either case, this membrane has to be flexible enough so that you can adapt to jobs, relationships, and careers. Review the following examples and think about when adapting is working well for the people described and when adapting appears to be stressful to them.

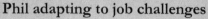

Phil adapting to job challenges

Phil, a young construction worker, scores extremely Direct on Scale A on his personal style profile. He is just slightly Direct, on this style in his work environment. However, he said that it is very stressful for him to be less Direct than he prefers to be.

Phil sees himself as a very take-charge, almost rebellious type of personality and he finds it very difficult to be the bottom man on the totem pole at work. Phil says he is constantly biting his tongue at work and not responding when someone corrects him because he knows that doing so would only get him into trouble. He is anxiously waiting for a time when he can be promoted upward and will not have to take orders from everyone else on the construction crew.

Work Style—Personal Style Worksheet

If your Work Style and Personal Style profiles are different, you are probably adapting to certain responsibilities, pressures, or stressors in one setting or the other.

If your work and personal profiles stay the same, this indicates that you behave consistently in these two environments. However, you may identify other settings where your behavior does shift, e.g., when making a speech, driving in rush-hour traffic, or receiving a performance appraisal.

Work Style Awareness

List some factors at work that may influence your behavior there and note whether the behavior is your natural style or a reaction to stress.

Example:
I become very Urgent at work because there are so many deadlines and emergencies. I am a slightly urgent, restless person naturally, but I turn this up a notch at work.

_____

_____

_____

_____

_____

Personal Style Awareness

List ways your Personal Style differs from your Work Style and identify some factors (people, pressures, responsibilities, etc.) that influence this change at home.

Example:
I am more Direct at home than I am on the job because parenting my two rather strong-minded teenagers requires that I be more forceful and controlling than I have to be at work.

_____

_____

_____

_____

_____

_____

_____

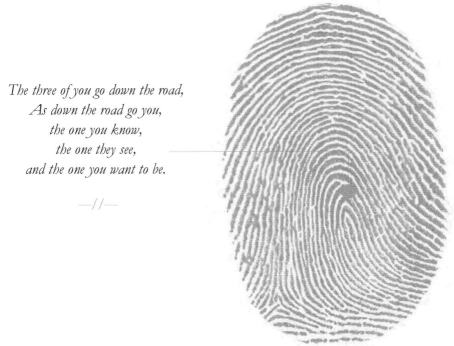

The three of you go down the road,
As down the road go you,
the one you know,
the one they see,
and the one you want to be.

—/ /—

PART 2:
"the one they see"

Others may see you differently than you see yourself. Perhaps they bring out a different side of you. Maybe the environment you are both in (work, home, school, recreation, etc.) influences your behavior and their perception. There may be certain responsibilities, deadlines, opportunities, etc. Your role as a leader can impact your actions and also their perceptions of you. Part 2 will help you explore "the one they see."

People may also see you differently due to their own personality traits. They may, in turn, behave differently around you and draw out certain reactions from you. Developing an accurate sense of how you come across to others is an essential component to leadership and team communication.

The road to self-insight runs through other people.

— David Dunning

In old English:
O wad some power the giftie gie us,
To see oursels as ithers see us!

— Robert Burns, 1786

—// —

Chapter 11

Learning how others see you

As the poem that guides the structure of this book points out, there is always that other person going down the road with you "...the one they see." This person is your "social identity" or "reputation." It lives in the minds of others. You can learn how others see you and even work to shape or reshape the impressions you have made in a positive manner that more closely aligns with your self-concept.

Imagine that people are all wearing sunglasses. They will each perceive you based on the color of the lenses they look through. The various ways they see you are all correct because they simply see you the way they do, from their unique perspectives. Their views, the colored lens they look through, can be influenced by their personality traits, job roles, relationship dynamics, personal familiarity, old memories, or even what others have told them about you.

Knowledge of how others see you will also help you understand their reactions to you and this helps you lead more effectively. You'll be better able to flex and adjust your behavior and consciously make changes that improve communication. In fact, awareness of how you come across to others is one of the keys to effective leadership.

Keep in mind, people have a right to their opinions. They develop their perceptions of you for a reason. This can, at times, be rather hard to accept. Learning their perceptions might even hurt your feelings. Your first reaction may be to think, "That's not right and they should be corrected." You might even get frustrated and say to yourself, "They can either like me or lump it." However, these types of reactions on your part don't solve anything and can even alienate others.

A part of developing strong relationships and enhancing your leadership skills is accepting the fact that others simply see you the way they do. Realize that the only way to change their perceptions is to change your behavior. If you have close relationships and frequent contact with people, you will be more likely to get them to see you differently. However, you'll have less impact with individuals that are more distant from you or less engaged with you on a daily basis. Changing their perceptions can be quite challenging. They have probably locked onto certain perceptions and will tend to resist letting go of these. It's human nature.

Even when you make an effort to change and you begin behaving differently, people tend to remember the reasons for their original perceptions. Changes to their views of you may come slowly. That's also a good reminder to invest time early in a relationship towards creating the relationship and impression you want, rather than trying to change a bad impression once it has been formed.

Learn from others

Sometimes others see your strengths more clearly than you do. That is an upside to learning about the perceptions of others. Work associates, teachers, coaches, grandparents, and close friends will each have a different line of sight and may see talents and potentials in you that you don't see. Stay open to their perceptions. You can benefit by embracing the positives that they see in you. Learn not to discount their views.

The goal is accuracy

You probably know some people who are rather self-absorbed and see themselves much more favorably than others see them. They may think they have only strengths and no weaknesses. However, they may just not be able to accept any weaknesses in themselves or they may not be able to admit being anything less than perfect.

Undoubtedly, you've witnessed the strain such self-absorbed self-perceptions can create in relationships. This can show up even in leaders. Unwillingness to consider other's perspectives and adjust to them can derail leadership efforts, stunt career success, blow up communications, and stress families to the breaking point. You don't want that to happen to you.

The *INSIGHT Inventory Observer Feedback* profile charts provide a great way learn about the perceptions of others. The scales are exactly the same as the self-rating assessment. When you ask someone to rate you, you learn more about yourself and the other person. This can point out communication issues related to personality trait differences and drive the opportunity to discuss important differences in perceptions.

Lessons from the past

The tendency to judge others quickly, almost instantly, is built into our DNA. In our ancient past, when humans existed in rather primitive tribes and clans, our survival depended on making fast accurate judgments of others. "fast and suspicious" of a stranger's intent was better than "slow and trusting" when it came to survival. Humans had to quickly decide whether a stranger was a friend or foe.

Humans could be fast and suspicious, yet wrong, and still survive. Slow and overly trusting could be deadly if our ancestors were wrong.

Judging the behavior of others—with a bias towards suspicioning the intention of others—was over generations programmed into our brains. This overlaps with judgments of different personality traits. When people are different from us our default "reactive" brain suspects the worse. Our thinking reasoning brain must learn to see the positives and strengths in differences.

Fortunately, most of us in our modern world have positive experiences with others. As leaders, we learn to see the advantages of differences in personality strengths and discover how different personality traits can complement and support each other. But, not everyone shares this value. Some people attribute negative qualities to various traits. That's why the "one they see" is important for you as a leader to learn about.

You may have heard the saying, "What someone else thinks of me is none of my business." This would be reassuring if you lived in isolation away from people, teams, family, and society, but few of us do. We need to know how we come across to others. This translates in part to comparing our self-perception of our personality traits to the perceptions that others have. Getting these to align closely is key to our communication success.

Developing an accurate perspective of how others see you is incredibly helpful, if not mandatory as a leader is mandatory since you are in charge of improving communication and transforming relationships. You cannot fully become the leader you want to be without this feedback. You may have a fairly good sense of how people view you, but you may not know how a specific person—who is important in your career—views you.

Obviously, it is good for your career to know how your manager sees you. It's important for your work performance to know how your coach or mentor sees you. Likewise, it is good for your love life to know how your dating partner or spouse sees you. You can expand this to any number of relationships; parenting, friendship, teaching, etc. Feedback is important.

Think of it this way, the more important the relationship is to you, the more critical it is to have accurate feedback on how you are perceived. Also, the bigger the difference between your self-rating and another person's view of you, the more important it is that you have a discussion about your differing perceptions.

As you review your *Insight Observer Feedback* profiles, remember that you carry a history of your self-perceptions that others don't have. For example, you may be aware that over time you have changed on certain traits. You may be very conscious of continuing to work on developing the positive attributes of a certain trait. The changes you've made, even the small ones, are obvious to you. However, others may not see these changes. They may think the changes are just temporary; therefore, they rate you based on their perceptions of the "old" you.

Another scenario might be that you consciously invest extra energy in flexing to communicate with particular individuals. You're sensitive to this effort and continuously aware of the energy it takes. However, those individuals may not have even noticed the changes you've made. A third possibility is that they are somewhat aware, but you've flexed this trait so long and so well that they see you only in this way. They may have forgotten that there is a different side to you. You will however, continue to be aware of your efforts at flexing and wonder why this isn't recogized.

A wild and crazy guy...or so he thought

Tom rated himself just slightly Precise at work on Scale D, Organizing. He really likes to have a place for everything and everything in place. His office is organized meticulously and he is confident that his systems and files help him work more efficiently. Tom rated himself slightly Unstructured at home in his Personal Style. He says he's been trying to be more flexible and less concerned about having everything organized.

However, when his teammate Kelly completed the *Insight Observer Feedback Rating* on Tom, she scored him very Precise, almost off the chart. In a lively discussion, Tom revealed that since he was trying hard to be less detail conscious and more spontaneous and flexible. He thought his efforts must be showing up at the office, and even at home. Kelly confirmed that this wasn't the case. Compared to her and others on their team—who were more Unstructured—he still came across as extremely Precise. However, she assured Ken that she and other team members appreciated his need for structure and wanted him to continue using that strength.

Being in charge here doesn't mean taking charge

As a new supervisor, Jay was extremely concerned that the crew he was in charge of would not respect him. The previous supervisor whom he was replacing was very tough and strong willed. It was his way or the highway. Jay saw his natural style of Influencing others (Scale A) as being Indirect. He was a believer in compromise, cooperation, and negotiation. But, driven by his fear that the crew would dismiss this softer style of leadership, he presented himself as very assertive, demanding, and autocratic.

Six months later when Sam, one of Jay's key assistants, completed the Observer Feedback Rating on Jay, he rated him as very Direct. Jay rated himself as very Indirect. Only after an open and honest discussion, and with Sam's feedback, was Jay able to see that he had created an image of himself that wasn't necessary. And it was backfiring on him. Some of the crew felt he was too demanding and unwilling to listen to other's ideas. In a way Jay was relieved to hear that he could move back to his natural, more Indirect style and still be effective.

Also, be aware that others may see you based on one or two memorable experiences from the past. Perhaps you were very impatient on a certain day and you irritated someone. Maybe you were very frank once and you hurt someone's feelings. Perhaps you were celebrating something one day and you were especially gregarious and outgoing. These memorable experiences can sear impressions into other peoples' brains because of their intensity. They may hold that image of you and not accept normal day-to-day behavior that doesn't support their earlier impression

One bad day can distort many good days.

Jason, a normally very Steady, patient, easy going individual was completely stressed one day at work. He had car trouble, learned that his apartment building was being sold and he'd have to move. Plus, he had been randomly selected for a tax audit. He was uncharacteristically on edge. A new person, Kendra, was joining his small entrepreneurial team to help brand and launch his newest invention. When she asked penetrating questions, he grew impatient, became defensive, and rushed to some poorly thought out decisions. Later, after working together for a year and experiencing Jason's normal calm, relaxed manner, Kendra rated Jason as Urgent and reactive on the Insight Observer Feedback assessment.

Jason was surprised and asked her about this and learned that his impatience and overreactions on Kendra's first day of work had made such an indelible mark on her memory that all the remaining days of the work year had failed to erase it. Kendra treated him as an Urgent reactive individual who was just having a number of "good" days since then, rather than as a Steady patient person who had just had one "bad" day. Jason and Kendra both learned how difficult it was to change a first impression, but agreed to be more open to day-to-day observable behavior.

Occasionally your self-perception may have seized up or become stuck on a self-image you developed in your head many years ago. You may struggle to accept that you have changed. You may still see yourself as that shy, awkward third grader and not fully embrace that you are now a successful, assertive, and confident professional. The Insight Observer Feedback profiles can be invaluable in helping you embrace the changes you have made.

Rediscovering her "true" self

Sammie grew up in a rather dysfunctional home with parents who abused alcohol. Her father, in particular, would become domineering and explosive. Sammie learned to be careful about what she said and how she said things. She never wanted to anger or upset him. Sammie herself was naturally very outspoken and direct. Over time, especially in her teenage years, she lost her voice and came across as shy and reserved.

Years later as an adult, away from her father's imposing and unpredictable presence, she began to regain her own identity and state her position on issues confidently and even forcefully in meetings. Her work team grew to appreciate her self-assured leadership style. However, Sammie still saw herself as shy and hesitant. She rated herself very Indirect and Reserved on the INSIGHT Inventory and found it hard to believe that her team members rated her on the Observer Feedback report as Direct and Outgoing. She found that her old self-image was clouding her view of her re-discovered, "true" self.

Then there are the perceptions of your friends. You may find that new acquaintances view you differently from some of your longtime friends who have a historical memory. These "old" friends may still carry a past impression of you that doesn't fit with your new behavior. Other long-time acquaintances, co-workers, and even friends may have difficulty allowing you to change because that requires adjustments on their part. They may keep you in a box that you no longer fit.

Time can stand still

Carson felt he lived two lives. He grew up diplomatic, quiet, studious, and quite reserved, some would say shy, in a small town. A late bloomer, he had few close friends and no dates in high school. In law school he discovered he had a knack for diplomacy and mediation. With his professor's connections he found himself on a fast pathway to international relations and US Embassy work. Within a few short years he was traveling worldwide and was seen by others as a confident, smooth, outgoing ambassador's legal assistant. When he met with world leaders in challenging meetings and was viewed by as elegant and "smooth." However, when he returned home for his 15-year high school reunion, his classmates still commented on how shy and awkward he seemed. He had changed and grown immensely and had made good use of his personality strengths, but for others time had stood still. They were unable to see anything except their original perceptions that had formed many years ago.

Learning how others see you

There are two options for obtaining observer ratings. The first method is to use the pages at the end of this chapter to ask others to create quick "guesstimates" of your personality traits. The second method is to use the online computerized system. It provides a way to purchase credits to invite others to rate your personality strengths and then save these in your online account.

Both options have their advantages. The online system provides more accurate ratings, compares your results with statistical norms, and saves them in a data base that you can refer back to at any time. The paper guesstimates are handy, quick, and provide instant results. They may not be quite as accurate, but they will help you initiate conversations with others regarding how they see you.

Whichever you choose—and you might decide do both—consider recording the results in this book on the pages provided. This will give you a quick resource to refer back to as you study other parts of this book. Plus, as time passes, it's often easier to find this book than to locate printed sheets that may get tucked away in a file somewhere.

Option One: The Observer Quick-Rate forms

If you choose to use the quick "guesstimate" forms, simply copy or tear out the charts in this chapter and begin. The people you request feedback from can review the short descriptions provided, plot their ratings of you on the chart, and connect the lines to create a feedback profile. You'll instantly have some feedback about your personality traits.

Be sure to share the results with the people who provided the rating. Show them your Self ratings and even the Observer ratings done by other people. This will help them understand the purpose of your request and will stimulate a discussion about your behavior and why it may be different around certain people. Remember, everyone is right!

Option Two: the online Insight Observer Assessment

You have probably already used the code on the last page this book to set up an account and complete the *INSIGHT Inventory* self-rating. You can go to customer service at the Insight Inventory website (www.insightinventory.com) and purchase credits for the online Observer report. These credits will be put in the same account where your SELF report resides. Using your same password and login, you will be guided through a process of inputting the names of the observers you wish to invite and sending them email instructions explaining how to do this. All email and personal information is held confidential and not shared with third parties.

The individuals you invite will rate you on exactly the same items as you rated yourself. The results will generate a chart showing how each observer sees you on the same four scales: Influencing,

Responding, Pacing, and Organizing. The descriptions will be positive and focused on your strengths.

Give the people you invite some time to complete the assessment. Then, check your account and review the results. If they have not yet completed the assessment, send them a reminder email and perhaps inquire if they have an email firewall or junk mail set up that may be blocking the invitation.

Quick-rate: Insight Observer Feedback

Feedback on (your name):

_____

Provided by (observer's name):

_____

Date: _____

Instructions: Ask the observer to place a large dot on each of the four scales below to indicate how the observer sees you. Then, connect these with a line.

INSIGHT Inventory

Plot how descriptive each trait is of this person

	very	moderately	slightly	slightly	moderately	very	

INDIRECT tactful, diplomatic, hesitant	[A] **Influencing**	**DIRECT** candid, forceful, confident, assertive
RESERVED quiet, introverted, solitary, few espressions	[B] **Responding**	**OUTGOING** expressive, talkative, animated
URGENT restless, decisive, impatient, seeks variety	[C] **Pacing**	**STEADY** patient, calm, easy going, deliberate
UNSTRUCTURED flexible, open, unstructured, disorganized	[D] **Organizing**	**PRECISE** structured, detailed, organized

Discussion Activity:

Compare the observer feedback to your self-rating.
Discuss any similarities and differences and what this suggests for communicating better in the future. List some actions to take below:

_____

_____

_____

Quick-rate: Insight Observer Feedback

Feedback on (your name):

_____

Provided by (observer's name):

_____

Date: _____

Instructions: Ask the observer to place a large dot on each of the four scales below to indicate how the observer sees you. Then, connect these with a line.

INSIGHT Inventory

Plot how descriptive each trait is of this person

	very	moderately	slightly	slightly	moderately	very	

INDIRECT
tactful, diplomatic, hesitant

A
Influencing

DIRECT
candid, forceful, confident, assertive

RESERVED
quiet, introverted, solitary, few espressions

B
Responding

OUTGOING
expressive, talkative, animated

URGENT
restless, decisive, impatient, seeks variety

C
Pacing

STEADY
patient, calm, easy going, deliberate

UNSTRUCTURED
flexible, open, unstructured, disorganized

D
Organizing

PRECISE
structured, detailed, organized

Discussion Activity:
Compare the observer feedback to your self-rating.
Discuss any similarities and differences and what this suggests for communicating better in the future. List some actions to take below:

_____

_____

_____

Quick-rate: Insight Observer Feedback

Feedback on (your name):

_____

Provided by (observer's name):

_____

Date: _____

Instructions: Ask the observer to place a large dot on each of the four scales to indicate how the observer sees you. Then, connect these with a line.

INSIGHT Inventory

Plot how descriptive each trait is of this person

	very	moderately	slightly	slightly	moderately	very	

INDIRECT tactful, diplomatic, hesitant	A Influencing	DIRECT candid, forceful, confident, assert
RESERVED quiet, introverted, solitary, few espressions	B Responding	OUTGOING expressive, talkative, animated
URGENT restless, decisive, impatient, seeks variety	C Pacing	STEADY patient, calm, easy going, deliber
UNSTRUCTURED flexible, open, unstructured, disorganized	D Organizing	PRECISE structured, detailed, organized

Discussion Activity:

Compare the observer feedback to your self-rating.

Discuss any similarities and differences and what this suggests for communicating better in the future. List some actions to take below:

_____

_____

_____

If you're going to say what you want to say, you're going to hear what you don't want to hear.
—Roberto Bolaño

If you're going to ask, be ready to change.
—David Maister

—//—

Chapter 12

Seeing How Others See

People will tend to judge you by your behaviors rather than your intentions. Yet, they probably judge themselves by their intentions rather than their behaviors. Therefore, watch your behaviors and be aware that they often reflect your personality trait tendencies, not necessarily your intentions at a given time.

This points out, yet again, the importance of knowing how your behavior comes across to others. When you behave a certain way, regardless of your intentions, you are vulnerable to the other person's judgment. Some people are understanding and forgiving; others are not. Remember, the definition of "insight" includes the ability to see yourself as others see you.

By nature, people tend to be "soft" on themselves but "hard" on others. They tend to justify and explain away any behavior that they didn't intend. However, it also means that they will frequently judge you with different standards than they judge themselves. Your behavior, in their minds, may be attached to a certain intention and they may be reluctant to be forgiving of behavior they see as inappropriate, harsh, or poorly thought out.

On the other hand, others may expect that you look beyond their behavior and try to identify all possible positive intentions. This means that as a leader, you'll need to stretch your ability to look deeper and try to uncover other people's good intentions before you make judgments about their behavior.

If you don't want to know, don't ask

Lucille is a very Direct and Urgent person. In an effort to be helpful, she gave her good friend Kip feedback regarding the presentation slides Kip had developed for an upcoming meeting. Lucille told Kip, rather bluntly, that the slide colors conflicted, the text was too small, and the sequence should be changed. This was intended to be helpful feedback. Kip heard the Direct feedback only as criticism and disapproval. Lucile was trying to be a candid, supportive co-worker, but because of the way she said things, not her intention, Kip entirely missed that Lucille meant to be helpful.

Our intentions are frequently misread because we do not attend closely enough to the behavior (body language, tone of voice, etc.) that we display when communicating. This can happen with behavior coming from any one of our personality traits. People may not see the strengths and may instead focus on the weaknesses that show up when strengths are overused or used at the wrong time. Therefore, it is important to be aware of possible shortcomings associated with each personality trait. The strengths of all the personality preferences and related behaviors, particularly if they are extreme, are suspect to being misread as weaknesses by people having opposite preferences.

Colored lenses

If you have red sunglasses on, everything will look rather pink and you will have difficulty seeing green since it is at the opposite end of the color spectrum. This doesn't mean the green doesn't exist, it's just that red sunglasses prevent you from seeing that color very well. In similar fashion, very Direct people may not see the strengths of very Indirect people, and vice versa. Both these opposite preferences view the world through different colored lenses. The same holds true for each of the personality traits.

This means that as a leader, it is very important for you to be aware of how others, particularly people who have the personality traits opposite from yours, may view you. It's also good to remind yourself from time to time, that you may view them inappropriately—perhaps even misjudge them—as you look through your own colored lenses. Review the following lists and check any negative judgments others may have made of you in the past. You'll probably find they were judging traits of yours and specific behaviors, not your intentions.

The best way to proceed is to select a couple of your most extreme personality traits and read the judgments frequently made about those traits. Your most extreme traits will most likely be noticed first and possibly judged negatively by others. The likelihood goes up when there are conflicts or misunderstandings.

SCALE A: Influencing

Misperceptions of the INDIRECT preference

As with all the preferences, challenges surface when a preference is overused. If you overuse your Indirect characteristics, you may find that other people, particularly more Direct, forceful individuals may see the weaknesses, especially when stressed or frustrated with you.

As an Indirect person, your:

- patterns of stating your position diplomatically may be viewed as lack of candor or even an unwillingness to be straightforward.
- efforts as coming across unassuming may cause you to be seen as lacking confidence.
- preference for negotiating rather than debating may be seen as unwillingness to stand up for what you truly believe.
- tendency to ask rather than tell may be viewed as manipulative rather than tactful.
- tendency to understate ideas may cause others to discount them.

List some additional "negative" feedback that you, as an Indirect person, may receive from time to time.

_____

_____

_____

_____

SCALE A: Influencing (cont'd)

Misperceptions of the DIRECT preference

You may find others, particularly very Indirect individuals, have the following observations of you, particularly when you're under stress and overusing your strengths.

As a Direct person, your:

- style of stating your position in a forceful, straightforward manner may be viewed as bluntness and intimidation.
- attempts at being candid and forthright may be viewed as harshness and insensitivity.
- efforts at coming across as confident may be seen as arrogance and self-centeredness.
- preference for getting unresolved issues out on the table and debated openly may be viewed as confrontational.
- tendency to "tell" rather than "ask" may be seen as domineering and autocratic.

List some other "negative" labels or critical feedback that you, as a Direct person, may receive from time to time.

_____

_____

_____

_____

SCALE B: Responding

Misperceptions of the RESERVED preference

You may find the following perceptions exist in others, particularly very Outgoing individuals. If you overuse your Reserved characteristics, you may find that others develop the following "negative" perceptions.

As a Reserved person, your:
- lack of animation and emotion might cause you to appear uninterested and disengaged to Outgoing individuals.
- aversion to big groups of people and being the center of attention may cause you to appear withdrawn or shy.
- inner focus on thoughts and ideas could come across as disinterest in people.
- discomfort with small talk might give the impression that you are not friendly or curious about others.

List some other "negative" or critical sounding feedback that you, as a Reserved person, might receive.

.

_____

_____

_____

_____

SCALE B: Responding (cont'd)

Misperceptions of the OUTGOING preference

You may find that others, particularly very Reserved individuals, may develop the following perspectives of you, particularly when you're overusing your style or under stress..

As an Outgoing person, your:
- enthusiastic expressions and friendliness may be seen as being superficial or even gushy.
- talkative, animated manner may come across as excessively emotional and even over-the-top to quiet, shy people.
- interest in people may be labeled insincere because others may think you can't possibly be as caring as you truly are.
- natural warmth and trust might cause you to appear to be gullible or lacking in discretion.

List some other "negative" or critical sounding feedback you, as an Outgoing person, may receive.

_____

_____

_____

_____

SCALE C: Pacing

Misperceptions of the URGENT preference

People, particularly Steady individuals, may view your strengths quite differently. This is especially true if you have recently rushed a decision and it turned out to be a mistake. Even when most of your decisions are good, a fast, poor one is seldom forgotten.

As an Urgent person, your:
- preference for considering only a few options and then deciding may be labeled as being impulsive.
- fast actions may be considered as recklessness.
- tendency to get bored quickly and switch to other projects can be perceived as a lack of persistence or commitment.
- quick reactions, especially when you are frustrated, can be labeled as impatience and lack of self-control.

List some other critical sounding feedback that you, as an Urgent person, may receive how it comes across as negative.

_____

_____

_____

_____

SCALE C: Pacing (cont'd)

Misperceptions of the STEADY preference

As a Steady, very deliberate person, you may find the following perceptions develop in others, particularly very Urgent individuals. As with all the preferences, when a preference is overused, particularly under stress, the extremes show up and others will notice them.

As a Steady person, your:

- preference for considering many options and deliberating before making a decision may be labeled as indecisiveness.
- ready, aim, aim, aim, fire pattern of making a choice may be labeled as procrastinating and delaying.
- tendency to work at a smooth, even pace can be thought of as dragging your feet or working slowly.
- understanding and easy going nature and may get you labeled as "too nice," and soft on difficult decisions.

List some other feedback you, as a Steady person, may receive that could come across as critical or negative.

_____

_____

_____

_____

SCALE D: Organizing

Misperceptions of the UNSTRUCTURED preference

Since you like to do things differently and follow your own drummer, you may find that Precise individuals, because of their need to adhere to rules and procedures, will be critical of your Unstructured manner at times.

As an Unstructured person, your:
- resistance to structure and order may appear to be challenging the systems that Precise people want you to follow.
- flexible approach to time could cause you to be late for meetings and get you labeled as inconsiderate of others
- inattention to details might make you come across as unprepared.
- pattern of letting things pile up before organizing them can cause a Precise person to perceive you as messy.

List some other critical sounding or negative judgments that you, as an Unstructured person, may hear.

_____

_____

_____

_____

SCALE D: Organizing (cont'd)

Misperceptions of the PRECISE preference

You may find that Unstructured individuals, because of their need to be flexible and work around what they see as unneeded rules, will be critical at times of your Precise, organized manner.

As a Precise person, your:

- attention to orderliness may cause you to be seen as obsessive and intolerant of how other people do things.
- need for detailed planning may cause you to be seen as judgmental of people having less organized approaches.
- attention to detail may get you labeled as a perfectionist and as a person who is overly critical and hard to please.
- preference for following rules and systems may cause you to come across as compulsive and inflexible.
- desire for others to follow your system may appear controlling and always wanting things done your way.

List some other feedback you, as a Precise person, may receive that could come across as harsh or negative.

_____

_____

_____

_____

The three of you go down the road,
As down the road go you,
the one you know,
the one they see,
and the one you want to be.

——// ——

PART 3:

"the one you want to be."

This section will help you become the leader you want to be. You'll identify ways to improve your communication skills, eliminate problem behaviors and change any negative thinking patterns to positive affirmations. Change doesn't come easily, yet if done in small increments, it isn't all that difficult and it certainly pays off big when leading others. A small redirection in the orbit of a satellite can result in a big difference in the trajectory and destination. Minor changes in the way you think and behave can, over time, take you to completely new places in your relationships and lead you down the road to becoming the person you want to be.

LEAD with INSIGHT

Be yourself; everyone else is already taken.
— Oscar Wilde

To be yourself in a world that is constantly trying to make you something else is the greatest accomplishment.
— Ralph Waldo Emerson

—//—

Chapter 13

Getting Seduced Out of Your Strengths

To get "seduced out of your strengths" means that you've been enticed by something appealing, desirable, and seductive enough that you have moved out of your personality strengths zone to gain the anticipated rewards. You may make these moves even when they cause stress and strain in your work or your personal relationships.

For example, you might take a new job for increased pay, yet soon find that the position requires you to use personality traits that are not your strengths. Perhaps you can flex your traits and perform the required tasks for a while, but it takes extra energy. These shifts may, over time, become increasingly difficult to maintain. You will most likely end up stressed and dissatisfied with your decision. You were seduced out of your strengths for higher income.

You can get seduced out of your strengths in any area of your life; not just career opportunities. You can be seduced by the trappings of leadership, power, and influence. You can be seduced by the excitement of a new relationship, the dream of raising "perfect" children or the possibility of living in a special location, etc. Many things that you desire can seduce you to trade off part of your "true self" to attain them.

Certain situations, relationships, and opportunities are a better fit for your personality strengths than others. You may settle in and succeed and yet start dreaming about other possibilities. By nature, human beings habituate quickly and some people in particular get restless and bored. When this happens, instead of fine tuning the strength and creating a plan for getting better at what you're already good at, you may make an impulsive change. This may cause you to take a job that may be wrong for you or commit to a relationship that isn't right and even restrains your natural strengths. When you discover a mismatch and you are experiencing stress and even health issues, then you have identified something that has seduced you out of your strengths.

Not relaxed working by the sea

Suzanne is Outgoing, loves people and groups. She is also very restless, impatient, and Urgent. These skills have made her quite popular as a rabbi to a large synagogue. However she always wanted to live by the ocean, so when the opportunity presented itself, she took a counseling position near a seaside resort. She soon found herself struggling with job responsibilities that prioritized the need to listen rather than talk, to be patient rather than rush into action, to be a coach rather than a player. She began to feel restrained and stressed, grew unhappy, and was physically sick more than she had ever been in her life. She was living in a beautiful location; but she was unable to enjoy it.

Suzanne eventually realized that the trade-off for the location where she dreamed of living and the poor job fit was not worth it. She had been seduced by her dream of living by the ocean at the cost of not using her personality strengths. It wasn't worth it.

After realizing this, she took a challenging job as an assistant director of a large, fast-growing spiritual community and began thriving again. She decided to use her personal time to take visits to an ocean-side vacation spot. The change of priorities and engagement of her true personality strengths revived and energized her.

In front of the podium

Ralph thrived as a software specialist. This position played to his Reserved, Steady, Unstructured personality traits. Most people would have considered Ralph to be well paid and living a comfortable and secure lifestyle. Ralph on the other hand, often felt unnoticed and underappreciated compared to his highly successful friends. So Ralph wrote a catchy book on software development and soon afterward he got the opportunity to take a speaking position and go on the road as a professional seminar leader. The pay was a nice increase, and it was incentive based. He earned more based on his efforts. Plus, it offered the prestige of getting in front of audiences and being admired.

Ralph started his new career with a bang, was very popular, and was excited about the possibilities. But, the software market changed rapidly, his expertise became somewhat outdated, and the travel was never-ending. The energy it took to charge up his naturally, quiet style to come across as animated, outgoing, and publically energetic every day began taking its toll. He was soon regretting his decision and realized he has been seduced out of his strengths by the allure of being famous and admired. It had cost him his day-to-day life satisfaction and work pleasure.

Both Suzanne and Ralph were seduced out of their strengths by rewards they thought they desired. For Suzanne it was the dream of living in a particular location. For Ralph it was increased income, fame, and prestige. The issue was not what either Suzanne or Ralph wanted, but rather that they chose pathways to achieve their desires that did not match their personality strengths.

Flexing for a short time is different from flexing for a long time.

It's fairly easy to flex your style a little bit for a short period of time. Most people have the capacity to do this. If you're Indirect, you can probably be more forceful and candid during an important discussion or heated debate. However, it is likely you won't find it easy to be Direct for an extended period of time, day in and day out, because this would require a great deal of self-management. Likewise, if you're Unstructured and you prefer things neat and clean, you may be able to flex for a short period of time and get your desk, storage areas, and garage all cleaned up and in order. However, you might not enjoy a job that requires constant attention to details, organization, advance planning, and other structured work.

Most people have to flex a bit in various areas of their lives. They may even develop skill at this. Flexing for a short time is not the same as taking on a permanent career role or being in a relationship that requires long-term commitment.

Ability vs. capacity

The ability to flex your personality strengths temporarily is different from the capacity to flex for a long time. If you get seduced out of your strengths, the issue becomes one of endurance. How long can you flex: days, weeks, or years? To adapt to a leadership role, different job, or new relationship that requires long-term flexing, you may have to flex more than you want.

Try to determine if what you desire is worth the effort to shift out of your strengths. Ask yourself if you are enjoying the challenge or actually increasing your daily stress? Bottom line, if you are stressed out at the end of the day—even though you're receiving the payoffs you wanted—you've probably been seduced out of your strengths.

Example: Jan seduced out of her strengths by a promotion.

Jan's Work Style before her promotion   Jan's Work Style afterwards

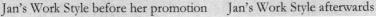

Jan was a successful software-programming specialist who preferred to work alone in a highly specialized area. Because of her exceptional work, she received a salary increase and flattering promotion to become a group leader. She debated the pros and cons of this change, but in the end she just couldn't resist. On her Work Style she scored Indirect, Reserved, Steady, and highly Precise. Her career as a technician had allowed her to work by herself or in small groups with minimal conflict and intrusion from others. She had a very secure, well-funded project that she had been involved with for many years. Her Steady, patient, persistent strengths fit those job requirements nicely. Jan's structured attention to detail and ability to document and track all project steps with precise high standards helped her stand out to corporate management.

The new leadership role she took required that she take charge of a rather disordered and independent thinking group of senior scientists. They had a pattern of challenging and debating everything and unfortunately took a rather cynical judgment of management. Jan was the first woman in the traditionally male department to take on the leadership role. However, Jan was smart and she knew how to flex her style and take charge. She shifted her normally Indirect style to a more Direct, forceful approach and moved forward confidently. She also flexed her naturally Reserved quiet style to a more expressive, talkative, Outgoing way of responding to her team. She reminded herself to engage in more small chats between breaks, talk to her team members frequently, and often stayed afterhours to discuss issues. Since Jan still had her engineering and design work to do, she continued with her Steady Precise style of making decisions and organizing her work. Even though others saw no drop in her organization, she felt she was letting things drop through the cracks because there was just not enough time in the day to manage others and still produce her work at the detailed level she was used to.

After a period of time, Jan started to wonder if the promotion had been worth it. She went home exhausted, found herself resenting the amount of time the leadership responsibilities took and grew weary over the amount of assertiveness she had to muster to ward off the challenges to her authority. This all added up to a new form of stress and she noticed she was eating more junk food and exercising less. Jan realized she has been drawn to the increased pay and the prestige of the leadership role. She intuitively knew that she was paying a price with her health and overall happiness. She had been seduced out of her strengths.

You may identify ways some of your life's experiences are similar to what Jan went through. The seductions may be different, the traits that you flex on may not be the same as Jan's, but the end point is very similar. You have to avoid getting seduced by rewards, money, and leadership temptations that require you to be different from who you truly are. Otherwise you will pay a price in terms of energy and happiness.

Identify the common seductions

The following examples point out the variety of ways you can be seduced out of your strengths. In reality, there is an endless list. One of your challenges is to become very aware of the opportunities; payoffs, rewards, etc. that are the most seductive to you.

The following list contains some examples of typical seductions. Check ones that might seduce you out of your strengths:
— fame and recognition

— money and financial benefits

— power and influence

— approval of others

— avoiding conflict

— parenting visions

— dreams of being the perfect grandparent

— life-style changes (retiring, relocating, etc.)

All of these seductive payoffs mean different things to different people. For example, "influence" may be defined by one person as political and encompass large groups of people, but for someone else "influence" might be limited to just being able to get your child to go to bed on time.

Not all seductions are the same

There are small seductions that may only temporarily move you out of your strengths. Then, there are larger ones that demand a lot of you. Some seductions are short-term, others will require years of investment.

Small seductions create only a little or moderate stress. You will probably find it fairly easy to break free of these. For example, you might volunteer for a role on a community organization or church group because you're seduced into being helpful and appreciated; the value behind this is a good thing. However, once you're in the role you may find that you're getting stressed rather than fulfilled. Although the mission may be meaningful, you may still find yourself not working in your personality strength zone. You may be asked to do detailed precise work and you're a big picture, unstructured individual. You may interface with many talkative people and you're really rather quiet and reserved. These are poor fits.

Ava's dilemma

Ava is Unstructured and Urgent. She's always pushing to try new things and she does get a lot done—fast! The parent teaching organization needed help with the launch of a new fundraising project for school supplies for disadvantaged students. The district office suggested she help even though she was hired as an assistant to the art and drama department. She found this very flattering and agreed to take on the role even though she wasn't an organized or detail oriented person. She prided herself on being a "creative type."

However, she soon found this position required attention to almost every detail, intense organizational skills, and careful navigation of many state regulations. She had to follow the book and it was a big one. She discovered that making things happen in fast creative ways—that matched her natural style—was not in this "job description." She soon became stressed out and miserable. She had been seduced out of her strengths by the flattering recommendations of her new manager. She wanted badly to quit, but hated to disappoint him because he had supported her drama department so generously

Outgoing stretch

Noland scored very Indirect and Reserved. This was a perfect fit for his executive coaching role. He often had to be diplomatic and tactful when dealing with oversized egos and gently ease them into self-reflection and change.

Nolan volunteered for his eight-year-old son's school spring trip. He had been told that it was very rewarding to go along as a parent. This was the type of parenting activity he envisioned taking time to attend. His own father had always been too busy, but he vowed to be a different type of parent. Besides, his coaching role isolated him from groups of people for long periods of time, and while he rather liked that, he thought it would be good for him to get out more.

However, once on the trip, Nolan's dream became a nightmare. He had to network and chat with the other parents, be enthusiastic around the kids, join sing-a-longs on the bus ride, and adapt to the loud, never-ending drone of the children talking, yelling, and just generally being young and energetic. He nursed a headache through the museums and tried to assure his son that he was "having fun." In the end, he vowed to spend more time in the future with his son in quieter, one-on-one activities. No more field trips! He had been seduced out of his strengths and recognized it.

Both of these examples were probably time-limited. The individuals described could identify how they were drawn out of their strengths zone, learn from the experience, and tell themselves that the next time they would choose their volunteer activities more carefully.

Watch out for the bigger seductions

Long-term decisions create bigger challenges to adapt and also reverse if they are wrong. Making a major career change that requires you to move away from a current role that draws on your strengths to a position that requires different traits but that you feel you could flex and manage, would be big. If the choice provides more income, then that may be seduction enough to cause you to believe you will be happier. However, if the tradeoff if not right and it involves others, family and friends, it will be more difficult to correct.

If a seductive promotion also impacts others in your family, such as moving to a new community where children must establish new friends, start at new schools, and begin life anew, then it's difficult to later accept the mistake and reverse course. Perhaps you would be able to pull off the amount of flexing that would need to be done; but the cost might be high in terms of your family's happiness and the stress and strain on your health.

At some point, on all important decisions, you'll have to decide if being seduced out of your strengths is worth the rewards obtained. If you decide "yes" then it will be important to identify coaching and self-development programs that help you learn the new people skills needed to succeed.

Fire the fire chief

Ken was a well-liked fire station chief. He was in charge of a small neighborhood fire station that was close to the home where he grew up. Ken's strongest personality traits were his tactful, Indirect style and his warm, Outgoing manner. Everyone seemed to like him immediately. Ken was also patient, very Steady and fairly Unstructured. He was always fair but was also willing to bend some policy manual rules to make sure his staff could attend family events. In a way, he was the perfect fire chief for the small neighborhood.

A big promotional opportunity came up for Ken to move to downtown and be the assistant fire chief of the large adjoining city. He had to flex his Indirect style and be more Direct, and come across as commanding, even domineering at times. This was quite stressful to him. Within a few years, Ken suffered a minor heart attack. He had become so stressed with the amount of flexing he had to do that he paid a price physically.

Luckily, Ken survived. After recovering, he took early retirement and moved with his wife back to their old neighborhood. He often wished that he had never left his old station. He had been seduced into taking on roles and responsibilities that weren't his strengths.

Seduced with your eyes wide open

The key take away is that you must know what you're giving up when you make a change to get something you want. When you're seduced out of your personality strengths, this means that you may give up behavior patterns that come naturally for you and that you're trading comfort for the challenge of flexing your style in order to attain other rewards. You may make the shift, learn new skills, and even enjoy the new opportunities that come from making the change. Other times, you may realize that the price you pay is too high and you'll want to return to your core personality traits where you can thrive in a less stressful manner.

Complete the worksheet and activity that follows to gain clarity and insight into decisions that may reflect seduction out of your strengths.

Strengths Seduction Worksheet

AWARENESS

List a time you've taken on something (task, role, or activity) that seduced you out of your strengths:

_____

_____

_____

UNDERSTANDING

What was the payoff for the tradeoff?

_____

_____

_____

ACTION

What changes would you need to make to get back to your strengths?

_____

_____

_____

Strengths Seduction Worksheet

AWARENESS

List a time you've taken on something (task, role, or activity) that seduced you out of your strengths:

_____

_____

_____

UNDERSTANDING

What was the payoff for the tradeoff?

_____

_____

_____

ACTION

What changes would you need to make to get back to your strengths?

_____

_____

_____

Strengths Seduction Worksheet

AWARENESS

List a time you've taken on something (task, role, or activity) that seduced you out of your strengths:

_____

_____

_____

UNDERSTANDING

What was the payoff for the tradeoff?

_____

_____

_____

ACTION

What changes would you need to make to get back to your strengths?

_____

_____

_____

> *It's not stress that kills us; it is our reaction to it.*
> —Hans Selye

> *The greatest weapon against stress is our ability*
> *to choose one thought over another.*
> —William James

—//—

Chapter 14

Spotting Stress and Strength Overuse

Nature built into humans the ability to fight, flee, fume, or freeze when faced with stress. These reactions helped us survive danger, injury, and even death. When you sense danger, real or imagined, your physiological system kicks in to ensure that you live through the threat. You experience this adrenalin rush first as a call to action, then afterwards as stress. In the modern world, low grade stress and unneeded vigilance, causes a slow exhaustion and lowering of performance. Most of your day-to-day fears aren't really dangerous to you; however, your body doesn't know this. It's going along for the ride, often an unpleasant one.

You're undoubtedly familiar with minor stress, the frustrating and irritating tension that often comes from the hassles of managing the ups and downs of daily life. These issues aren't life and death threatening, but they can build up and cause chronic stress. Whether a meeting runs longer than you expected, your pet has gotten sick, or an unpleasant family member wants to visit, it may seem that everywhere you turn there are pressures that limit your ability to achieve your priorities. These intrusions and unexpected interruptions translate to generalized stress and anxiety.

There is also another type of stress; the situations or interactions that inhibit you from using your personality strengths. You experience "personality trait" stress when you find yourself in situations that prevent you from being your natural, true you. When you have to move out of your strengths zone and draw upon other behaviors, this takes energy because it goes against your natural inclinations. As you develop more skill at flexing the degree of stress decreases, but at first these adaptations require effort and consume energy.

Stress over time

Heidi is an office manager and she's very organized and Precise. She makes it a priority to adhere to schedules. When she attends meetings that are poorly managed and go on and on, she becomes frustrated and stressed and gets critical of the meeting leader. She thinks to herself about the necessity of certain agenda items, the disrespect of peoples' time, etc. At the worst meetings she makes herself almost physically sick. Her Percise trait paired with her tendency to be critical leads her to wish others were more like her. She carries this irritation and stress home and it wears on her family members. Heidi becomes her own worst enemy.

Style overuse

Stress also arises from not being able to get things you want or do things in your preferred way. These two block the achievement of results and lead to strengths overuse. At those times you may do more of what you're already good at doing. This is like an exaggeration of one or more of your personality strengths. Each of the personality traits has an overuse pattern.

When you're under stress your brain tends to respond by using more of the super highways of thought and old patterns you are already good at doing. Therefore, it's easy to slip into strength "overuse." For example, under stress, Steady individuals will frequently fall into a pattern of seeking more options and delaying decisions. They hope subconsciously that this extra time will eliminate the stress of choosing, unfortunately just the opposite occurs. The delay brings about other problems and more decisions.

In a similar fashion, Indirect individuals may resort to conflict-avoidant patterns when stressed. This probably worked in the past to eliminate the tension between themselves and others. They build a neural highway for avoidance. However, when they say "yes" when they should say "no" their avoidance of conflict may result in more stress.

Breaking stress overuse patterns involves learning to remove yourself from the situation, observe yourself from a distant perspective, and then mindfully respond rather than mindlessly react. Sometimes this is called gaining a view from 50,000 feet and then intentionally choosing the most appropriate response.

Gain a new perspective.

The following pages on personality trait stress will help you identify:
1) what you are likely to do when under stress
2) ways to select alternative behaviors that might work better
3) how to not take other people's overuse patterns personally

While it may be helpful to read through it all at some future point, to get started, just select one or two of your most intense personality traits. Then, review the appropriate section on overuse of those traits. Later come back and read other sections. As a leader you'll want to learn the patterns that other people display and how to be most helpful at those times.

OVERUSE SCALE A - INFLUENCING

Overuse of INDIRECT strengths

INDIRECT

Stressful situations: being confronted and drawn into arguments; having others take advantage of your tactfulness and compliance.

Reactions: you may avoid conflicts and disagreements, or give in when you don't really agree.

As an Indirect person, when you move out of your strengths zone you'll tend to lose your voice, avoid conflict at any cost, and try to please people, perhaps by saying "yes" when you want to say "no." You may believe this makes it easy for others to work with you; however, this trait overuse can actually be challenging, particularly for more Direct individuals. They may not feel they can candidly bounce ideas off you or push back against your position without having you give in and agree just to decrease tension. This can actually be uncomfortable to them.

Another pattern that you may find yourself engaging in is silence. This means that you simply don't speak up, commit yourself, or put a stake in the ground when discussions become emotional. This has an immediate a payoff for you. You avoid conflict at least for the moment. However, the secondary cost is that others may conclude that you are unwilling to join in and fully participate.

When you do get upset with someone, you may have to watch that you don't take your concerns to a third person rather than speak frankly to the person you are upset with. Or, you might be tempted to use email or social media, anything to avoid a face-to-face confrontation. This can actually make matters worse and cause you to come across as secretive or even passive aggressive. While you postponed conflict, you may actually cause other tensions to increase.

People pleasing backfires for Sharon
Sharon designed backdrops for scenes of a local theater. She was known for her conflict free, easy-going, Indirect style. Then, Leif, the mild-mannered producer of the playhouse retired and was replaced by Addison, a young, confident, and Direct individual.

Leif, the previous producer, had always trusted Sharon and gave her team complete independence in creating the scenes. However, Addison wanted everything done certain way and he would become agitated and frustrated when anything went wrong. Sharon was stressed by this and instead of debating things with Addison she started to question her work, and needlessly check in on small things.

Sharon became so focused on pleasing Addison that she abandoned her own judgment, compromised her designs, and ended up pleasing neither herself nor Addison. The constant strain of appeasing Addison became very stressful and Sharon eventually quit without discussing her concerns. Addison was shocked, not realizing that it was Sharon's unsuccessful efforts at gaining his approval that had caused her to quit her job. He thought she was doing great.

Eating alone is not always stress free.
Gilbert always went to lunch alone. His co-workers began to think that he didn't enjoy their company. But, the reality was quite different. Gilbert grew up in a home where conflict was avoided at all costs. His parents were so Indirect they didn't argue, they just kept their frustrations to themselves. He learned the same pattern. The fast growing company work setting was just the opposite. He began eating alone to escape what he believed was conflict and this was actually creating conflict. He eventually flexed his style and stayed engaged and it helped improve communication even though he remained uncomfortable at times.

Overuse of Direct strengths

DIRECT

Stressful situations: not being able to voice opinions; not knowing where you stand; loss of authority and influence.

Reactions: may get demanding or become argumentative and overly forceful to regain control.

As a Direct individual you will be stressed when you find yourself losing control over a negotiation, feeling diminished in influence, or getting nowhere in a debate. This is made worse if you don't feel you can present your side of an issue or challenge decisions made by people in higher authority.

To gain more influence you may move to a telling and controlling mode of communicating, the very thing you yourself dislike. But, it will come easy to you because it's a small shift to go more extreme on the Direct trait. Unfortunately, this can result in heated arguments that are more about power than ideas or positions.

Information is also a form of control. You prefer working in settings where you continually know where you stand and there are clear pathways to moving up in authority. You do best when given frank and candid feedback; but you'll have to watch the tendency to disagree and argue with it if it doesn't fit your self-image.

As a Direct, assertive and confident person, when under stress you'll move toward dominance, control, and forcefulness. You may not notice how tough minded you can be and you may even believe you are just being a strong, take-charge leader. Others, particularly Indirect people, can find you to be very difficult to deal with, even intimidating. They may not speak up or worse yet, they may do what they think you want even when they see problems or mistakes coming that could have been prevented.

Tom's overuse of Direct

Tom enjoys debating, trying legal cases, and arguing his side. He seems to be a perfect fit for a career in trial law. Tom is very Direct and quite charismatic when in front of juries. He confidently presents his client's cases and convinces juries of the merits of his arguments.

However, Tom often finds himself working alone with few other attorneys willing to work with him. His colleagues report that Tom frequently comes across as pushy, overly confident, and even arrogant. Legal assistants who work for him come and go, usually leaving when they feel Tom was overly demanding of their time and critical of their efforts. Some have even accused him of being emotionally abusive and an office bully.

Tom is always shocked by such feedback. He feels he is only focusing on the tasks at hand. He feels when employees are hired, they know they are working for him and will have to do things his way. He doesn't see the need for team-building or communication training because he sees others as having problems with authority, not him. Unfortunately, when he overuses his strengths, he pays the price in employee commitment, turnover, and loss of teamwork.

Coach without a Team

Weston was a star on every softball team she's played on. However, now as an assistant coach, she switches teams almost every year. She is very direct and candid and if she doesn't like a play her head coach calls, she challenges him. While she feels she is just being a strong and vocal leader, the head coaches see her as argumentative and disrespectful. When under stress, Weston defaults to an even more extreme Direct mode and starts "yelling and telling." She longs for the day when she can be in charge and make all the decisions herself. She doesn't realize she'll need to learn to be a team oriented coach first and put the relationship before winning.

OVERUSE SCALE B - RESERVED AND OUTGOING

Overuse of RESERVED strengths

RESERVED

Stressful situations: dealing with too many people; pressure to talk a lot in groups or be entertaining.

Reactions: may withdraw, become excessively quiet, or hold back thoughts and emotions. May not speak up when contributing would be helpful.

If you scored Reserved you will be stressed by intense stimulation whether it be loud music, people talking, or excessive activity. While everyone needs downtime away from noise and stimulation, as a Reserved person you will need more sooner and for longer. If you go past your tolerance point you may find yourself shutting others completely out and begin to feel rather alienated. This is the "alone in a crowd" sensation that can actually be quite isolating.

Because of your quiet nature, people may view you as disengaged or even disinterested in either them or whatever is going on. This may not actually be the case, but remember reality is in the eye of the beholder. Outgoing people look for visible cues of engagement such as eye contact, talking, animation, expression, etc. If they don't see these, they have trouble believing you are interested and involved.

As a Reserved person you may find that you're frequently over-stimulated by high levels of activity and large groups. To ground yourself you probably have learned to turn inward and shut out the sounds and interactions of others. A typical reaction under this stress will be to overuse your Reserved nature and move away from people, quit talking, and find ways to be alone or just with one or two close friends. This "shutting down" may help you but it can strain relationships. Therefore, try to track the impact of your behavior on others, particularly Outgoing people, and find ways to engage a bit more.

Partying differently

Jenny just couldn't understand her law partner Max. Even with his reserved, quiet, low-key approachable manner, Max would initiate conversations with strangers when he was at professional meetings. But, when a large legal conference was arranged Max would quit talking and not even stay very long at meet and greet cocktail gatherings.

After several such occurrences, Jenny could see it coming; Max would start out involved; but, as the laughter, energy, and background music grew louder, instead of getting energized, Max would appear to grow dazed and disinterested. After a certain point he would tune out and quit talking almost altogether.

Sometimes Max would even excuse himself and move to an unused meeting room to read a book. At first Jenny thought Max was growing disinterested in the profession and their thriving practice. However, she learned that he was reacting to the stimulation of large groups of people much differently than she did. There was a certain moment in every gathering where enough was enough and Max would feel over-stressed and needed time away.

A wild and crazy office birthday party, not!

Grace hit a milestone birthday. Suzanne, her very outgoing secretary envisioned a large party with lots of co-workers, customers, and even ex-employees to celebrate the occasion. Suzanne was shocked to learn that Grace instead wanted only a small dinner with her small team. Suzanne reluctantly arranged it. Grace however, was thrilled and announced that it was the best gift ever—quiet, small, and meaningful—just perfect she said.

Overuse of OUTGOING strengths

OUTGOING

Stressful situations: lack of people contact; loss of affirmation and group support.

Reactions: may talk excessively, try too hard to gain approval, or come across as overly friendly.

If you scored Outgoing on the second scale you become stressed by lack of people contact, the feeling of separation from others, or the loss of affirmation from members of groups that are important to you. At those times, you will be driven to rebuild relationships and connections with others. To do this, you may invest effort making contact; phoning friends, logging into social media, and whatever it takes to renew your connections with others.

Frequently this will work. Others will see your efforts as an expression of your friendly, outgoing style. However, you may be aware that when you're feeling stressed you tend to develop a compelling need to be liked by others. At these times, you may overuse your strengths by talking too much, becoming inappropriately friendly, or even coming across a bit superficial.

You may find it shocking to think that anyone could ever view your outgoing nature to be a problem. However, remember that half the population scores Reserved and ten percent of them score very Reserved. These individuals may not relate to your talkativeness and intensely friendly manner because it is so foreign to their way of going. That's why some will be guarded and suspicious of your intentions. They may think you want something from them or that you're lobbying for attention. On the other hand, others will love your gregarious nature; just be sure to maintain a balance.

The wind beneath Laurie's wings.
Laurie and VJ run a small advertising agency. In addition to being business partners, they have been best friends since childhood. Laurie is extremely Outgoing. When at her best, her strengths lead her to meet many customers and her vivacious energy easily wins over new business. At local networking events she has a talent for going in unknown and leaving as the center of attention.

However, VJ has seen the vulnerable, more insecure side of Laurie appear when she has become over stressed. Regardless of how many customers their firm has, Laurie can begin to worry that others don't really value and appreciate their services. At those times she will start calling and reconnecting to assure herself that she is still liked. Unfortunately, when this behavior is driven by stress rather than positive energy, it comes across as insecurity.

VJ has never wavered in her support and friendship with Laurie. She has seen this pattern surface before and knows that Laurie is a caring and wonderful person. VJ waits out these periods of insecurity and is there by her side when Laurie rebounds.

Brian on stage
Brian is naturally very Outgoing. He makes friends with everyone he sees. When he took a new job he tried to build new relationships fast, perhaps too fast. His manager Carl was used to walking into the work area and having all eyes and attention on him. However, when Brian arrived first, he would introduce himself to others, crack jokes, and put the focus on him. Soon Carl began to feel that Brian was trying to overshadow him. Brian's overuse of his Outgoing trait caused problems when he tried too hard to be the center of attention. He learned he had to pull back at times and let others be noticed and appreciated.

OVERUSE SCALE C - URGENT AND STEADY

Overuse of URGENT strengths

URGENT

Stressful situations: lack of action, slow decision making; changes in situations that cause delays.

Reactions: you may get frustrated and impatient or make impulsive decisions.

If you scored Urgent on Scale C, you like to take action, hate to wait, and become frustrated by delays. Therefore, when your need for quick decisions and speedy action is thwarted, you'll tend to get impatient and begin rushing, pushing, or even snapping at people in hopes of bringing about action. These stress reactions rarely solve the problems leading to the delays and can irritate others and cause them to react back with defensive remarks. When this happens, the situation only gets worse and things take even longer.

Delays and stress can also cause you to make hasty, impulsive decisions. You are probably making these quick decisions as a way to move forward and get on with things. You may feel that any action is better than no action. However, this fast decision-making can lead to a "ready, fire, aim" mindset. You get ready quickly, you pull the trigger on your decision fast, and then once you see the result you rethink the quality of the outcome. Even if your aim was off and you didn't get the outcome you wanted, it may have felt good to move ahead with things.

When you decide based on impatience, rather than information, you may not allow time to identify the best information available. This action may have temporarily minimized your stress, but it may lead to other unforeseen problems. If others become upset with you, you'll have to watch that you don't blame others for taking too long. They will see that as a poor excuse targeted at them.

Driving the side roads

Kendra works in a crowded area of a large city. Although her daily commute is manageable and not excessively long, it still pushes her right to the edge of her patience because it involves slow-moving bumper-to-bumper traffic. When traffic gets particularly snarled, Kendra gets impatient. She admits that she's a horn blaster. She says it helps her drain off frustration. But this behavior has backfired for her and strained relationships with car-pooling co-workers.

When delayed, Kendra will frequently pull off the main road and head up and down alleys, through bike lanes, and across parking lots to try to cut ahead in traffic. She says she feels better keeping her car moving even though she goes a long distance out of her way. Unfortunately, she usually runs into some unexpected roadblocks or other problems. Typically, her cross-country efforts cost her more time than she would have spent patiently waiting in traffic and her co-workers get to work stressed after the hectic drive.

Let's get going

Marcum works at a community kitchen volunteering to deliver meals to house-bound seniors. His food preparation team appreciates his high energy. When he's on, he gets the work of two people done. However, when he is overly stressed he gets so impatient that he will jump in his car and leave the center with only part of the meals they hoped he would deliver. On those days, he accomplishes half as much. He laughs and says he'd rather come back and go out again rather than be delayed double checking the entries. It's just too frustrating to wait he says.

Overuse of STEADY strengths

STEADY

Stressful situations: pressure to make fast decisions; last minute deadlines; frequent interruptions.

Reactions: you find ways to postpone decisions, delay taking action, and block interruptions.

As a person who scored Steady on Scale C, you will probably be stressed by pressure to make fast decisions on issues that you have not had time to think through. If you have enough time to consider the options and do your homework: i.e., looking at the pros and cons of all the choices, weighing alternatives, etc. you can make good decisions. But, if the decision is a new or particularly difficult one and you have not yet had time to explore the possibilities, then you will want to take your time and think things through.

Other people may try to help by pushing you to decide. "Come on." "Hurry up." "It's no big deal, just decide." However, added pressure usually does not help you move your process along; in fact, it may hinder it. You may try to please them to reduce the pressure and then actually become derailed from your own thought process. This can delay things more and make matters even worse.

Overuse of the Steady preference is sometimes labeled, "ready, aim, aim, aim, then fire." This is an exaggeration of how you behave but may reflect how others view your behavior. Steady people sometimes get very stuck and invested in collecting more information than needed. Then they get analysis paralysis and can't take action on any one of the choices available.

Remember, the time it takes to make a decision doesn't always reflect the quality of a decision. Although you may believe the extra time helps you make a good decision, there are some Steady people who take a long time and end up making poor decisions. Be sure to use time to collect good information and not get distracted.

Pressure can cause delay

Kenya a Steady, deliberate individual tends to take a lot of time making decisions and moving toward action. She works as a vet tech at an animal hospital. Her personal dentist, Ryan, is long term customer and Kenya knows all his pets. Ryan's dog developed an infection and when treating him, Kenya learned that there were two options. The veterinarian was out and Kenya had the authority to decide which alternative to pursue. She weighed the pros and cons, but just couldn't choose.

As she waivered hoping to make the right decision the day grew to a close and Kenya was forced to select the only option left, an antibiotic wash and cleanse. The dog recovered fine, but it took a couple of extra days. Kenya felt badly that she hadn't made a quick decision and gone with medications. She had become stressed over the need to make a decision and had gotten paralysis by analysis.

Where to eat

Mabry hates it when her team leader, Connor, requests a working lunch and then asks her to select a restaurant. She finds herself put on the spot when having to choose a place to eat. Connor believes he is being polite by asking. However, his direct, urgent manner feels to Mabry like pressure and impatience. She would prefer to have some prior notice so she can think about places to recommend, but when pressed she just picks a place, any place, to relieve the pressure. She then fumes and blames Connor for being a poor leader and getting irritated when she makes a poor decision. Those meetings get off to a bad start.

OVERUSE SCALE D - UNSTRUCTURED AND PRECISE

Overuse of UNSTRUCTURED strengths

UNSTRUCTURED

Stressful situations: too many policies and procedures to follow; lack of flexibility, and little support for doing things differently.

Reactions: may work around rules and not attend to details and schedules that are important to others.

If you're Unstructured, you like to keep your options open and your schedule "unplanned." You'll tend to resist systems and structure, and will postpone attending to small things. When under stress, you'll tend to overuse your Unstructured characteristics by dropping the details of life, i.e. paperwork, due dates, application deadlines, etc. Bills may go unpaid, license plates can expire, and various minor commitments fall between the cracks. You may also run late to meetings, forget to turn in papers or projects, and miss deadlines.

A big part of modern society relies on people attending to rules, policies, and procedures. So, when you're stressed and missing details, you're going to cause stress to both yourself and also any Precise structured individuals in your immediate surroundings. Remember, they are trying to get things ordered and organized. They will think of you as the problem rather than part of the solution.

If you work in a traditional, somewhat conventional setting, particularly large organizations or military service branches, you may find their structure comforting at first. You know what to do, when to do it, and what the rules are. However, when you come under stress and want to do things differently, you'll start to resist and struggle at following those very systems. There can be an internal cost, you may start to disengage and daydream about having a job with more freedom and flexibility. You'll need to monitor your capacity to work within institutions with lots of rules.

Austin's real education

Austin was an Unstructured English major and excited about his new graduate assistantship. He was finally going to get a chance to teach a freshman class and continue his graduate studies. He was selected because of his flexibility and creativity. He got off to a good start winning over the students with his flexible schedule and open-minded approach. However by mid-semester as the class progressed, complaints were beginning to flood into the dean's office.

Austin overused his unstructured style and would shift randomly from one textbook to another. He did not schedule assignments in any sequential plan and he often sprang pop quizzes in an unpredictable manner. While some unstructured students thrived in this classroom environment, most of them were lost and unsure of how to succeed. Austin's overuse of his Unstructured style created the very problem he most hoped to avoid, conflict! The Dean responded to the complaints by asking Austin to provide detailed, structured lesson plans and have these pre-approved and posted two weeks ahead of class time. Austin's dream job had become a nightmare.

Freedom, nothing left to lose...but a dream

Delores is Unstructured and Sam is Precise. Both are entrepreneurs with a big shared dream, but they have quite different approaches to operations. Delores wants to take things as they come while Sam wants everything ordered and organized ahead of time. Delores admires his expertise, but finds his style "boring." Sam worries that Delores will do something unpredictable or fail to attend to an issue and put their business at risk. Their opposite preferences are both their strengths and weaknesses as partners.

Overuse of PRECISE strengths

PRECISE

Stressful situations: ambiguity and lack of organization; poor planning; unpredictable change.

Reactions: may become more organized than needed or overwhelm others with details and lists.

If you scored Precise, you seek order, strive for organization, and attend rigorously to details. These are all good strengths. However, when you become stressed your tendency will be to do more of what you're already good at, organizing and striving for perfection.

However, when stress gets the best of you, you may start re-organizing what you've already organized, nitpicking little things, and obsessing over details that are not really all that important. You may even find that you start cleaning and filing things to distract yourself from issues that are bothering you.

Your overuse patterns of perfectionism and orderliness can wear thin on others. At those times, you may come across as difficult to please and overly critical. Your preferred ways to do things can seem to be unimportant and even irritating to others. If you insist, it can cause others to feel over-controlled by you. They may feel they have to work or live under your "watchful" eye and that a zero tolerance policy is in place.

Creating more rules to follow is one form of control. Another is setting such high standards that others feel they can't reach them. While these rules and procedures may help relieve stress for you, they actually create tension in others. They may worry that you'll find something wrong with their work or the way they did things. They may even resort to hiding information from you or doing things when you're away. Since you're probably more likely to be a perfectionist when under stress, you'll have to watch that you don't become a "stress carrier" in the eyes of others.

By the clock

Dave, a very Precise, organized team leader tries to be very punctual. He gets stressed by meeting start-stop times. In a special meeting he called, it became apparent that it would take longer than the hour he planned and he knew this would ruin the schedule he had in place for the evening. He overreacted by cutting the meeting at exactly the termination time even though an important decision was just minutes from being made. Sticking to the time frame felt more important to him at that moment than accomplishing the result the meeting was set to achieve.

Dave later regretted not allowing just a little more time. It would have saved him much more time down the road because he had to recall the team and almost start over. In the situation, he had grown agitated, started clock watching, and overused his Precise structured preference to reduce his momentary stress.

Cubical for two

Ava and Emily share a cubical at a health care service center. Ava is Precise and prides herself on efficiency. She keeps her desk space clear, files her paper work daily, and checks her to do list religiously. Emily on the other hand is lucky to find a space on her area of the desk to put her coffee cup. She piles folders up and seems to always be dealing with emergencies. Ava and Emily generally get along great but the differences in organization creates conflict at times. One solution that has helped is that set up a divider that separates the cubical desk into two sections. That simple idea really helped.

Monitor your style overuse

Communicating with others, working in teams, coping with family members, etc., all involve interactions riddled with potential misunderstandings that lead to stress. When tension develops, most people default to nonproductive strength overuse. This can be problematic because it causes you and your reaction to appear to be the problem rather than the issue that is causing the stress. Increasing your awareness of the connection between your personality strengths and your stress reactions will help you learn to manage your reactions and avoid being a "stress carrier." In addition, it helps you be truer to yourself by not turning your strengths into weaknesses.

Positives of stress

Stress can be positive, at times. Identifying why you're feeling stressed and how that relates to your personality strengths can be extremely helpful. You can learn to avoid the situations that cause the stress in the first place, or you can identify ways to deal with these situations differently.

Stress causes most people to overuse their strengths, and if this happens to you, it can wear you down, sapping much-needed energy that you could use for something productive or helpful to others. Getting better knowing when you're stressed by tracking the over use of your strengths can actually help alleviate the stress. It helps you become more aware of the process and allows you to choose your responses rather than be controlled by strong reactions.

Once you get a handle on how different situations or behaviors push you out of your strengths zone, you can learn how to modify your own responses to stay in your comfort zone. Part of becoming who you want to be in life is to understand what stresses you and then to manage it more effectively before you overuse your strengths. A good question to ask yourself when under stress is "Who is showing up instead of you." It's probably the person others see but not who you want to be. You can change this.

Stress Overuse Worksheet

Controlling style overuse allows you to stay within your strengths zone and use your strengths.

AWARENESS

List possible pressures or stresses that may relate to overusing your style.

_____

_____

_____

UNDERSTANDING

List trait overuse that is related to the stresses listed above.

_____

_____

_____

ACTION

Refer to your personality strengths and list replacement behavior that you can use in the future.

_____

_____

_____

Stress Overuse Worksheet

Controlling style overuse allows you to stay within your strengths zone, and use your strengths.

AWARENESS

List possible pressures or stresses that may relate to overusing your style.

_____

_____

_____

UNDERSTANDING

List trait overuse that is related to the stresses listed above.

_____

_____

_____

ACTION

Refer to your personality strengths and list replacement behavior that you can use in the future.

_____

_____

_____

Stress Overuse Worksheet

Controlling style overuse allows you to stay within
your strengths zone, and use your strengths.

AWARENESS
List possible pressures or stresses that may relate to overusing your style.

_____

_____

_____

UNDERSTANDING
List trait overuse that is related to the stresses listed above.

_____

_____

_____

ACTION
Refer to your personality strengths and list replacement behavior that you
can use in the future.

_____

_____

_____

Stress Overuse Worksheet

Controlling style overuse allows you to stay within your strengths zone, and use your strengths.

AWARENESS
List possible pressures or stresses that may relate to overusing your style.

_____

_____

_____

UNDERSTANDING
List trait overuse that is related to the stresses listed above.

_____

_____

_____

ACTION
Refer to your personality strengths and list replacement behavior that you can use in the future.

_____

_____

_____

The best cure for one's bad tendencies is to see them in action in another person.

— Alain de Botton

———//———

Chapter 15

Eliminating Trait Triggers

Has someone ever done something, perhaps a relatively minor thing, and for some reason it caused you to overreact and get frustrated, upset, or even angry? Then, later as you thought back on the incident, you couldn't quite explain the intensity of your reaction. Or, have you ever seen someone, who was normally cool, calm, and collected, just blow up unexpectedly? If so, it's likely you witnessed a personality trait trigger.

Triggers and hot buttons are the instantaneous and often subconscious overuse of one or more of your personality traits. Trait triggers pull you out of your strengths zones and lead to extreme reactions. Since these are so intense, they can strain and damage relationships. Triggers are challenging to catch and eliminate because they tend to pop up so quickly that you may not be aware of what caused them or stop yourself before you react. Plus, the psychological roots of hot buttons and triggers may be so established that they have come to seem normal to you. Co-workers, friends, and family may have learned to avoid tripping them, or worse yet have adjusted to them and just define these triggers as part of who you are. With insight, awareness, and understanding, you can figure triggers and hot buttons out, replace them with more effective behavior, and rebuild the relationships they have strained.

The first step is to identify your trait triggers. They are different from the style overuse patterns that surfaces more slowly under stress. Triggers and hot buttons are hotter, more explosive, and often unpredictable. Plus, they often hide out in your subconscious. You may not be fully aware of why you get triggered and react the way you do. They frequently take people by surprise.

You may not even be aware of just how sensitive you are to the behaviors or situations that trigger you. Your reactions can stem from situations in your past, perhaps in childhood, and they may have grown out of coping strategies you developed years ago. When activated, triggers override your personality strengths. Instead of being at your best, you react in ways that strain communication, blow up relationships, and disrupt teamwork.

Again, it is the speed and specificity of your trigger reactions that separates them from personality strengths overuse (as covered in a previous chapter). Strengths overuse usually has some early warning signals and takes a period of time to manifest. A trait trigger, however, is an instantaneous reaction to a behavior or situation. A specific gesture (such as sighing, staring, or pointing) or a comment that came across a certain way (criticism, personal discount, blaming, etc.) can ignite an explosive reaction. The same Indirect person described in the previous example could instantly react to a disapproving sigh by shutting down, leaving the room, and walking away from the discussions with a huff. The trait trigger strains the discussion immediately or even brings it to an end. Triggers and hot buttons are rarely productive or helpful. Part of "becoming who you want to be" involves identifying your triggers, hot buttons, and anger outbursts and actively working to control these and replace them with more positive appropriate responses.

Examples of trait triggers

Sometimes triggers and hot buttons are reactions to what others might consider relatively meaningless behaviors. They can be different for different people. If people raise their voices and start yelling, this may trigger a fear reaction in one person, but a flash of anger and defiance in someone else. Both individuals might have a "trigger" around yelling because they share a similar past experience of feeling helpless as a child, but their reactions may be quite different.

If someone expresses displeasure through silence, this may trigger irritation and an emotional shut down in you because it reminds you of a disapproving parent early in your life. But, with someone else, the silence might trigger intense frustration and cause them to make snide and cutting remarks. Since different people react to different things, your initial challenge is to focus on your reactions, not the triggers, and learn to spot them first. You can begin by creating a list of your triggers and hot buttons.

The following list will help you get started. It identifies some behaviors that can lead to trigger reactions:

- eye-rolling and looks of disinterest
- finger-pointing and provocative gestures
- heavy sighing and exasperated breathiness
- walking away and door-slamming
- glaring eye contact
- smirking or mocking facial expressions
- raising voice or yelling
- blaming or critical remarks
- sideways glances
- frowning or scowling
- whispering and commenting behind your back

- talking over the top of you when speaking, etc.
- avoiding you, looking the other way

Take time to create a list of some of the behaviors that trigger anger, frustration, and emotional outbursts in you. Use the form provided on the next page. Most people find they can list two or three triggers fairly quickly, but then they go blank. If this happens, think about some small irritants. Go smaller rather than larger. Everyone has many triggers and hot buttons, but they become so embedded and familiar that they feel normal. You'll also find that the little hot buttons can trigger bigger ones, so there is value in listing anything that comes to mind even if they seem insignificant at first.

Another strategy is to work through this list with others who know you well. They may see triggers that you aren't aware of. Some of these are actually funny and rather unique to you. Identifying them, and having a good laugh or two, can help you learn to spot larger ones. This list will give you lots to work on.

IDENTIFYING TRIGGERS and HOT BUTTONS

Create a list of behaviors, actions, or situations that trigger emotional reactions or anger outbursts in you.

_____

_____

_____

_____

_____

_____

_____

_____

_____

Any of the behaviors you listed can pull your trigger or push your hot button. It's important to note that triggers and hot buttons are actually neutral. This may be difficult to believe because some are so frequently shared among people in certain age groups, cultural segments, communities, etc. All the same, they take their power from you and the meaning you attach to them. One way to spot this is to note how certain behaviors or situations may garner almost no response in a friend, yet will bring out an intense reaction in you. Start watching others, reviewing other people's hot-button lists, and observing people and you'll gain a new perspective on triggers and yourself.

Don't Yell

Patricia and Andrea are both triggered by the same thing, yelling. Patricia is Indirect and Reserved and grew up in a home where her parents rarely argued. When they disagreed, they gave each other the silent treatment. Patricia learned to react to anger by shutting down. When someone yells she freezes up and is unable to speak her mind. Andrea on the other hand, who is Direct and Outgoing, gets very intense and agitated. She grew up in a volatile, loud, outgoing home. When she is around someone who yells, she reacts by raising her own voice, yelling back, and charging into the confrontation. Both Patricia and Andrea have triggers around yelling, but they are completely different. Neither learned reaction helps them be effective leaders when co-workers or clients get angry and yell.

If you step back and analyze the triggers in the example, you'll notice that both Patricia and Andrea are triggered by the same behavior, yelling. But, they react in opposite ways. In many ways, their reactions mirror their personality traits. This is a frequent pattern. Many times the clue to a trigger can be traced through a personality preference. This topic is further explored in the following sections so keep your profile in mind and see if you can trace any of your triggers and hot buttons to some of your personality traits.

Our trigger-laden past.

To better understand trait triggers, it may be helpful to step back and examine triggers from our evolutionary past and compare these to our modern-day emotional triggers. They are frequently linked.

Historically speaking, physiological triggers saved our lives. Our ancestors had to survive harsh and often dangerous environments. They needed to avoid both large predators that could eat them and small creatures that could poison them with a bite or sting. They even had to be on the watch for other humans from distant tribes or groups. One unguarded moment could lead to a life-ending injury.

Early humans developed physiological triggers that helped them react instantaneously to physical threats; the large predators, dangerous situations, and poisonous creatures. Certain sounds, i.e. growls, snapping sounds, buzzing, rattling and various sensations, i.e. tickling feelings running across their faces or necks etc., became hard-wired in their brains and triggered instant reactions. This made it possible for humans to respond with such life-preserving reactions such as jumping, ducking, smacking, screaming, etc. without the need to consciously stop and think about the level of danger. It was usually better to be safe than sorry; to react rather than think.

Even today, eons later, we still react quickly to loud noises, suspicious sounds in the night, or the sensation of an insect or spider crawling across our necks or faces. With lightning speed, we scream and swat at the sensation and run and hide from loud threatening sounds.

Physiological cues trigger instant emotion in us and an adrenalin rush that makes it possible for us to physically react without taking the time to consider and ponder too many options. The speed of our reactions may not now be critical for survival. However, these physiological trigger reactions remain with us from our distant past having been hardwired in our brain. They lie in wait ready to rescue us when needed. Unfortunately, our brains often fire up and our bodies gear up for the wrong reasons in modern day life. This can cause undue stress and bodily fatigue which in turn can cause us to say and do the wrong things at times without thinking.

Emotional survival leads to trait triggers.

Mental triggers can occur equally as fast as physiological ones. Rather than being purely instinctive, psychological triggers and hot buttons tend to have a large component of learned behavior. They are frequently linked to your strongest or most intense personality traits. They subconsciously cause you to react to what other people say and do. These reactions probably protected you psychologically earlier in your life from some challenging or dysfunctional family, school, or relationship dynamics.

Now, if you experience behaviors that remind you of some of those old dynamics—even years later and in a completely different situation—your brain may still go instantly to your previously learned emotional reactions. You get "triggered" and then react by exploding or overusing your strongest traits.

Because of your early learning experiences, you were hardwired in your childhood to react to certain stress-inducing behaviors, sights, or sounds with near-instantaneous speed. You learned such things as displaying anger, fleeing, avoiding certain encounters, freezing up, etc. Now in adult life, when triggered in normal situations such as work groups, team dynamics, family gatherings, community groups, etc., those old learned reactions can surface instantaneously. When they do, they throw you out of our personality strengths zone, strain relationships, and disrupt communication. Plus, they put stress on your friends, coworkers, and family members and frequently trigger a counter reaction in them. You trigger their triggers.

What's wrong with triggers and hot buttons?

On the upside, triggers and hot buttons provide psychological safety nets and the near instantaneous reactions may protect you from some old relationship dynamics. But, on the downside triggers come with a cost. Triggers and hot buttons pull you out of your strengths and draw you into negative patterns of relating (explosiveness, distrust, control, avoidance, etc.) and nonproductive behaviors.

Why you use triggers.

You use triggers and hot button reactions because they work even when there is a price to be paid. Perhaps you want to get others to stop engaging in a certain behavior, defer to your wishes, leave, give up, or some similar result. If you pull your trigger and blow up, yell, snap back, blame, etc., your reactions are likely to cause others to comply with your wishes. Granted, people may resent your behavior and be upset with you (that's the cost), but if they comply in any way, this reinforces your triggers and hot buttons. They worked.

When self-rewarding isn't really rewarding.

Trigger reactions and hot button outbursts can also become self-reinforcing. Anger, emotional explosions, or sarcasm can give you a moment of pleasure and a feeling of power. This can be subconscious and people often deny that they obtain any pleasure from becoming angry. However, if you ever hear someone say something like, "Wow, I blew up and let them have it and it felt great!" or "I just clammed up and quit. That really taught them a lesson!" You are hearing someone describe secondary rewards they received from the behavior. These often contain moments of power and a feeling of self-satisfaction.

If some of these descriptions sound familiar, think carefully about what reinforcement you may derive from a trigger. Even though the sense of power or momentary satisfactions feel good, in the long term they aren't actually "rewarding." People may label you as hot-headed and explosive and then quit trying to please you. They may start avoiding you or describe these outbursts to others in derogatory ways. This isn't what you really want and it certainly isn't really rewarding. Plus, once you become known for your triggers and hot buttons it's difficult to change people's impressions.

Don't trigger someone else's trigger

Be careful that you don't get caught in a destructive pattern of triggering other peoples' triggers. When you overact with a trigger outburst, a blaming comment or critical remark, you may trigger a strong counter-reaction in another person. This is called triggering someone's trigger. These patterns can cause a back and forth cycle of explosive reactions between the two of you. Sometimes other people watching and listening even join in.

When you trigger someone else's trigger, communication worsens, rather than improves. Anger outbursts turn into verbal and sometimes even physical fights. Criticism shifts into a back-and-forth blame game that neither party can win. Avoidance can trigger aloofness, aloofness can trigger indifference and soon there can be an unbridgeable gap between people. Bottom line, triggering other people's triggers makes matters worse. The first step in breaking this cycle is to become more aware of your own triggers and learn to control them.

Rolling eyeballs

Katherine had, since her teenage years, developed a habit of rolling her eyes and sighing when she disagreed with others. This didn't seem to irritate her college friends or family. But, when hired by a small company, the owner, Stan, had an old trigger related to this very behavior. For him, eye rolling was a sign of disrespect. In the first staff meeting she attended, Katherine thought Stan was pointing a project in the wrong direction. She rolled her eyes and sighed when she was asked to help.

When Stan saw this behavior, it triggered his direct, urgent personality trait extremes. He demanded she pay attention and not question his experience. He eventually got so worked up he just fired her on the spot, in front of the other employees. Katherine didn't even know what she had done. Stan was so angry that he couldn't explain to the team why he fired her so quickly.

The eye-rolling behavior was such a strong trigger for Stan that he went immediately to an extreme emotional reaction on his part. Rather than trying to discover what had set him off and learn how to better manage his reaction, he simply fired Katherine. He just couldn't seem to control his reaction. Katherine rolled her eyes and uttered a "whatever" and left, totally clueless about what she had done. They had triggered each other's triggers. Unfortunately, neither learned what had occurred.

Here is another example, finger wagging. It is a fairly common trigger and a behavior that is often learned or shared in certain ethnic communities and subgroups. It frequently triggers strong reactions in others.

Finger wagging trigger

Dave's trigger is having someone point and wag their finger at him. When someone is trying to make a point in a debate and shakes a finger at Dave's face, he flares with anger and explodes with heated accusations and insults. This doesn't work well, but this trigger has been ingrained in him since childhood. He remembers that whenever he would make a small mistake, an older stepsister would critically shake her finger at him, criticize him, and say humiliating things. He learned that the only way to stop her was to get angry and blow up. Now, years later this trigger continues to erupt at even the slightest indication that someone is being critical and especially when they point a finger. It causes problems for him and he hasn't made the link back to the historical cause.

It is fairly apparent how certain triggers are related to personality traits, past experiences, or a combination of the two. Reactions in childhood often carry over into adult life.

Don't be late

Karen has a trigger when it comes to tardiness. This relates to one of her personality trait strengths. Karen is both Direct (candid, frank, and blunt) and Precise (structured, organized, and timely). When others arrive late to meetings she gets triggered. She becomes very irritated and will openly criticize them as they take their seats. Her trigger pulls her into overly controlling and excessively judgmental behavior. Since Karen hasn't learned how to identify and control this trigger, co-workers have adapted by showing up early or, if running late, just skipping the meeting altogether to avoid being the target of her anger. Everyone loses, particularly Karen. She blames others for poor planning. The other co-workers blame her for being overly critical about minor tardiness and hot headed rather than considerate. Triggers have been triggered.

Breaking the Cycle: Awareness—Understanding—Action

Trait triggers and hot buttons can be eliminated or at least controlled. This process starts with becoming more aware of your personality strengths, a step you began when you completed the *INSIGHT Inventory* and have been developing throughout this book. Once you know your strengths, you have a positive reference point to return to once you eliminate problematic triggers and hot buttons.

Unraveling triggers can, at first, be rather discouraging. You may discover you have a lot of triggers; the average person does. You might even believe that you have more problematic patterns than positive ones. This is not the case. However, because the process of untangling triggers and hot buttons feels like you're focusing on the negative and it frequently brings up intense feelings. It is easy to become derailed and feel you have more challenges than strengths. Don't be discouraged. The following three-step process will help you eliminate triggers and bring you back to your strengths zone.

Step 1: Awareness

Almost any time you're quickly thrown out of your personality strengths, there is a trait trigger or hot button lurking in the background. Developing a broader awareness of your triggers is the first step in reducing their negative impact and eventually eliminating them.

Noticing and catching your trait triggers early in a stressful interaction, right when extreme reactions begin to emerge, provides the best opportunity for you to stop and redirect your thinking. This will help you eventually change your behavior. You can't change behaviors you're not aware of. Then, increase your awareness of the intensity. Some triggers do little harm to relationships, but others are so intense that not only do they damage and strain the communication with the person who pushed the trigger, your reaction may create fallout and impact others in the office, witnesses, and even people who hear about it second hand at a later date.

Also, try to spot the timing, the specific moments when you moved out of your strengths and snapped over to your trigger reaction. You might find it helpful to ask for help from others who observe you frequently. Friends, co-workers, and family members certainly witness your triggers on a daily basis. They probably see triggers you are not even aware of. This is normal because you will be caught up in the moment, the unfolding and the drama of your trigger reactions. It can be difficult to step back at those times and see what you are doing. But in time, you can learn from their feedback and become more observant.

Watch out for blaming. When something triggers you, your tendency may be to blame your over reaction on the behaviors of others. "They made me do it!" "She set me off." "He knows I don't like that." Yes, they provided the stimulus, but you unleashed the reaction. So, your first step in increasing "Awareness" is to learn to spot your own role in any emotional outburst. You have to learn to see your trait triggers for what they are. Your triggers always impact others and often escalate the negative in interactions and communication. Becoming aware of your personality trait triggers amounts to taking responsibility for your reactions. As a leader, you're also a role model so it is particularly important for you to develop the most awareness of your triggers and hot buttons.

Step 2: Understanding

Next, you need to understand, at least at some minimal level, where your triggers developed and be able to trace them back to some of their original sources. This historical understanding does not need to involve any deep psychoanalysis; it is not therapy. Simply discovering some of the original influences will serve to point out that many of your trait triggers developed for a reason. They are not random or happenstance; nor are they shared by everyone.

To explore the origination, ask yourself: Where did this reaction happen before? Why am I so sensitive to particular gestures, voice tones, and body language? Where in your past did this reactivity originate? When did this begin? How far back did it get started?

It's important to see that triggers had their benefits and payoffs in the past when you originally developed them. Certain trait triggers may have protected you from excessive criticism by helping you shut down and not personalize harsh or emotionally painful feedback. Other trait triggers may have helped you avoid being bullied at school. You may have learned to disappear, fight back, or give in to aggressive behavior. Perhaps you learned to be a "people pleaser" to avoid criticism from others. When did it start? With whom?

If you grew up in a poorly functioning family, trait triggers may have helped ensure that your voice was heard. Perhaps you learned to yell louder than the other screaming voices. On the other hand, you may have mastered the art of becoming invisible to escape some irrational and explosive anger. Or, you could have learned to complain about every little inconvenience as a way of connecting with a parent who was lost in a negative, constantly overwhelmed state.

There are as many examples and possible reasons for developing hot buttons and triggers as there are triggers. Some hot buttons are more problematic than others. Not all triggers are created equal.

Some are apparent and others have been suppressed and are challenging to unravel. Some triggers occur frequently; others only show up in special situations. This is normal. Welcome to the human race.

Resolving one trigger doesn't mean that the others are fixed by default. You'll need to tackle them independently, one-by-one. Sometimes when you eliminate one hot button, another may surface. Don't get discouraged. Trigger by trigger, hot button by hot button, you will gain skill in eliminating your triggers. As you resolve them you'll develop strategies that will help you work through other triggers more quickly. You'll develop a new skill set, "trigger elimination mastery," that will serve you well throughout your life and help you transform your relationships for the better. You're on the road to becoming the person you want to be.

Don't be ashamed of your triggers! Embarrassed a bit yes, motivated to change yes, but not ashamed. Remember, you developed each trigger for a reason. They may have been misdirected and not the ideal choice, but they may have been the best you could do at the time. Now, use your creative energy to retrace where and when those triggers developed and eliminate them for good. Then, replace them with more appropriate behaviors in line with your current values.

Step 3: Action

Take action. Trait triggers need to be dealt with. Don't leave your trait triggers unaddressed; they will only worsen. Some hot buttons even seem to increase with age and stress as the years go on. The last thing you need are more difficult relationships as you age. It's better to become known for your personality strengths, not for your hot buttons and triggers. Action involves replacing the trigger with a new more reasonable behavior. Ideally the replacement will be related to a personality strength of yours and a conscious decision to use it more often in the future.

For example, instead of raising your voice and yelling at someone who has disappointed you and triggered an old sensitivity, you may choose to be more patient and explore what really happened. Pause and then intentionally develop a more appropriate response. Or, instead of sitting back and saying nothing when a conflict erupts, you may choose to add your voice to the discussion, present another perspective, and take responsibility for moving the conversation toward solutions that will be supported by everyone. This creates opportunities for dialogue rather than extending the problem through an old pattern of silence and inaction.

Instead of returning an insulting gesture from a driver on the roadway, you may choose to ignore it, let the driver move on, and then congratulate yourself for relaxing and not escalating the situation. This puts you in charge, not the old hot button. Triggers can be replaced with constructive behaviors that reflect your true personality strengths.

Implementing the change cycle

Making use of the three step change cycle—Awareness, Understanding, Action—will help you reduce, if not eliminate many triggers and hot buttons. You can do this. It's not always easy, but sometimes it's not all that difficult. Some triggers will be easy to identify once you know what to look for. Then, you can move quickly through awareness and get right to action if you have a clear direction of what replacement action you want to adopt. Equipped with forgiveness, humor, and insight, most triggers can be minimized if not eliminated.

Here's the process. When you catch yourself moving out of your personality strengths and overreacting to something, find a way to stop. Break the pattern. Pause long enough to identify what it was that triggered you to become upset or react so intensely. Look past the actual events or words that were said and identify what they meant to you.

For example, perhaps a family member asked why the water hose had been left running so long. Suppose your reaction was to become angry and return fire with some defensive challenge, "Well, why are you asking?" or blame others, "It's not my job to watch over the water hose; it was Joe's!" Instead, take a pause. During the time out, notice that it wasn't the particular situation or words that were used that triggered your intense reaction, but rather the feeling that you were being blamed for something. So now you have the trigger, "When I feel blamed, I get defensive." Or "When I feel blamed, I transfer the accusation to someone else."

Next, trace this pattern back to an earlier experience in your life. Perhaps as a child, you felt blamed for mishaps around the house by one of your parents who were particularly perfectionistic and quick to make critical, blaming comments when things went wrong. Maybe as a powerless child you suffered in silence, but now as an adult whenever you feel blamed for even the smallest of things, your sensitivity causes you to get loud, defensive, and argue back. Or, perhaps as a child it worked to transfer the blame to one of your siblings and make a fast escape. Now, you may catch yourself repeating this pattern to an unlucky bystander. Whatever the case, the original reaction worked to some degree for you as a child. It helped you escape some discomfort. But, now you can create a more appropriate response.

The new response you select will replace your old reaction to being blamed. Perhaps you'll say instead, "Wow, thanks for pointing that out." or "I wonder how that happened?" or "It looks like the plants have enough water now and it is the perfect time to turn it off." No blame, no defensiveness. You'll then be able to move forward and turn off the water and put away the hose and not feel you have to defend yourself, look for someone else to blame, yell back, etc. You'll find that the new replacement action brings you more peace, causes fewer problems, and soon becomes more rewarding on its own. Plus, you'll feel much better about yourself.

It's also helpful to ask friends and family to help you catch some of your triggers and provide feedback on their responses to you at those times. They'll probably welcome the chance. Perhaps they've even been waiting for quite some time for the opportunity to bring these up for discussion. You can learn more about yourself and perhaps set an example that they want to follow.

Share your triggers and hot buttons.

There is something magical about the willingness to identify and share your triggers and hot buttons. It makes it possible for others to see your behavior from another perspective. They may even start to see their own triggers. When you admit to having triggers and participate in unraveling your hot buttons with friends and family, everyone benefits. Learning what each other's triggers are and discovering how to avoid setting them off, improves relationships. Plus, when you know some of the history behind one another's triggers, each of you will become more forgiving, understanding, and willing to navigate around each other's hot buttons.

Friends, family, and coworkers can also learn from you, how to respond to your triggers. If you're the person with the trigger, who is better qualified to teach others what to do than you? You can identify the responses they could practice that would be the most helpful in bringing you back to your strengths. You can advise others on whether they should say something, say nothing, take action, or just wait it out. Knowing what to do will be very relieving to them. Hearing from you and then knowing what you want them to say will help both of you get past your next trigger.

Summary

The cycle of eliminating trait triggers involves Awareness, Understanding, and Action. First, you must become aware of your personality strengths and the connected trait triggers. Then, you need to gain a deeper understanding of how your trait triggers developed.

Finally, you'll have to create a list of more effective responses to choose from. These are particularly powerful if they relate to your personality strengths. Take some time to trace back several trait triggers. This will help you catch them earlier each time they surface and modify them before they derail you and bump you out of your strengths zone. Then, practice this as a component of becoming who you want to be.

Use the following activity sheets to get started eliminating your triggers and hot buttons.

Eliminating Triggers Activity

Use this three-step process to become aware of your triggers and hot buttons, understand where they come from and replace them with actions reflective of your strengths.

1) AWARENESS

List a trigger or hot button you have caught yourself using:

_____

_____

2) UNDERSTANDING

Identify any learned reactions or past memories that may have led to this.

_____

_____

_____

3) ACTION

Refer to your personality strengths and list the replacement behaviors that you would rather use in the future.

_____

_____

_____

Eliminating Triggers Activity

Use this three-step process to become aware of your triggers and hot buttons, understand where they come from and replace them with actions reflective of your strengths.

1) AWARENESS

List a trigger or hot button you have caught yourself using:

_____

_____

2) UNDERSTANDING
Identify any learned reactions or past memories that may have led to this.

_____

_____

_____

3) ACTION
Refer to your personality strengths and list the replacement behaviors that you would rather use in the future.

_____

_____

_____

Eliminating Triggers Activity

Use this three-step process to become aware of your triggers and hot buttons, understand where they come from and replace them with actions reflective of your strengths.

1) AWARENESS

List a trigger or hot button you have caught yourself using:

_____

_____

2) UNDERSTANDING
Identify any learned reactions or past memories that may have led to this.

_____

_____

_____

3) ACTION
Refer to your personality strengths and list the replacement behaviors that you would rather use in the future.

_____

_____

_____

Two great talkers will not travel far together.
— Spanish Proverb

"Between the stimulus and response there is a space.
In that space is our power to choose our response.
In our response lies our growth and our freedom."
— Viktor Frankl

—//—

Chapter 16

Flexing Your Style

Flexing means to temporarily change and modify your behavior to more closely match the behavioral style of the person with whom you are communicating. It involves choosing to use a style preference that will resonate with the other person, even though it may not be your preferred style. All relationships are give-and-take with giving required before taking. To be a good leader and communicator you have to flex before you can expect others to flex.

A metaphor from the world of personal fitness might be helpful. Suppose you're competing in the decathlon, a competition that requires success in ten different events. To do well, you have to demonstrate how physically fit and skilled you are in each area. You need to be able to swim, run, jump, hurdle, throw, etc. Plus, you have to be balanced; if you are weak in any one area you will be less competitive and less successful.

Emotional fitness, the ability to communicate with a wide range of people is similar. You must be able to adapt and flex to communicate with a variety of people. As a leader, if you wish to work well with a variety of people (and not just one or two) you'll want to acquire a wide range of versatility in flexing with different people.

Developing skill at flexing your personality preferences makes it possible for you to be successful with people whether you're leading a team, connecting with friends, or dealing with family. You temporarily shift your behavior in the direction of the person you are communicating with. This is particularly important in times of stress or when there are big issues to resolve.

It's tempting to wish that others would flex their style and move in your direction and adapt to your behavioral and communication preferences. Wouldn't that be great. The reality is this doesn't happen as often as it should. Most individuals communicate in ways that are comfortable to them and are relatively unaware of the impact their styles have on others. This is where the opportunity lies. If you become effective at flexing your style, you will be seen as a good communicator. You'll always be part of the solution rather than part of the problem. This gives you the power to make any conversation, any relationship, a good one.

Types of flexing

There are two types of flexing. First, there is flexing to communicate more effectively with people whose styles are opposite from yours. This type of flexing requires you to shift your behavior patterns and behave in a manner somewhat similar to the other person's style. Second, there is flexing to communicate better with people who are similar to you. When you and another person have the same style, the challenge is to avoid overlaps that might cause the two of you to move to non-productive extremes. In this form of flexing you intentionally behave somewhat differently from the other person. You work to introduce different thinking and behaving to insure you and the other similar person consider a wider range of options.

Flexing is a work in progress.

Flexing sounds easy. How difficult can it be to modify your behavioral style a bit? Well, it can actually be rather challenging. When interacting with others, you'll tend to instinctively resort to your primary trait preferences. These preferences are naturally comfortable to you. However, they may not always be the best behaviors to use in certain situations and with particular people. On the other hand, choosing not to flex can make you an accomplice to every communication problem you encounter. It's always better to be part of the solution rather than the problem. This takes work and it's something that continues throughout out your life. The good news is that as you progress in your skill, flexing becomes easier and easier to do. At some point it will become so automatic that it becomes a positive character attribute that others will appreciate in you.

But, I like myself just the way I am.

You may have heard someone say, "I am just the way I am." or "I've worked hard to become me and I'm not changing." Yes, it's important to value your strengths. However, flexing isn't about changing who you are. It is about expanding your range and stretching your versatility when communicating. Don't get held back by thinking it means to stop being your true you. You can be who you are and still be good at flexing.

Likewise, try not to say, "I'll change after the other person changes." Your responsibility as a good communicator is to go first. Besides, if you put your success in the hands of other people, you'll be waiting a long time. Instead, look for opportunities to flex your style first and initiate change before the other person does. Don't keep score, don't wait on others; be active, not passive. Over time, flexing will become a skill and something you do naturally.

Again, by definition, flexing is actively choosing how to respond to other people's personality traits and behavior. Consciously, mindfully, choosing your responses makes you an active rather than passive communicator. The next step is to choose the timing of when to flex. Flexing takes place in the pause between the stimulus and response.

Suppose someone is very Direct and Urgent and that person says something that seems to be pushing you to take action. If you happen to be Indirect and Steady your immediate reaction may be to feel imposed upon or even criticized. Pausing after the other person's behavior and thinking through the situation allows you to see that the behavior is more about the other person than it is about you. You'll pause and think "Hmmm...most Direct Urgent individuals get declarative and impatient particularly when under stress." You won't react, but instead say to yourself, this is something to discuss at the "teachable moment." This pause makes all the difference. The more aware of choosing your behavior the better and more effective you will be.

Flexing is giving.

An important personal value underlies the action of flexing. If you are willing to flex your style to make communication with others easier, you are putting the relationship first. You are a person who places relationships with others ahead of your personal needs. You are saying, "I value this relationship so much, I will take the first step and flex my style to help ensure that the communication between us is positive and productive." By initiating action, rather than waiting for the other person to flex, you are making the relationship a priority. Yes, flexing takes extra effort, that's why flexing is an act of giving.

What to flex first?

Your score on any trait could fall anywhere from the far left extreme to the far right on each of the four scales in the *INSIGHT Inventory*. With four independent traits, this creates many possibilities for your profile shape. The person you flex your style to communicate better with also has an equal number of profile possibilities. Given the thousands of potential combinations, the challenge of flexing can seem overwhelming.

There is an easy way to identify what trait(s) to flex first on. Usually, the most extreme trait differences between you and the other person are the ones that initially cause tension. They are the strongest and most likely to get overused when under stress. Therefore, identify the traits you and the other person are the most different on and flex those traits first.

The second way to determine what trait(s) to flex is to identify the communication problems that are occurring and link these back to trait differences. These traits are probably contributing to the misunderstandings. For example, if tension is around timeliness and organization, take a quick look at Scale D, Organizing. If the problem is around the speed of decision making, consider Scale C, Pacing. Perhaps one of you is Steady and the other person is Urgent. Try to tie the problem to a personality trait where you are different from another person and flex on that trait first.

Similarity on a trait can also lead to misunderstandings between people. Consider the issue of timeliness and orderliness. Two very Precise, structured individuals may both have a high need for organization, but each may be very confident that their way of organizing things is the "right" way. It may be very difficult for either person to agree to follow the system the other person recommends because that would mean giving up their preferred method. One of the two will have to flex to avoid a conflict.

One trait isn't more problematic than another. It's frequently assumed that two very Direct, assertive individuals will have the most conflict because they can both move quickly to telling rather than asking. However, disagreement surfaces, at least as often among very Precise individuals who have differing ways of doing things. It can be quite challenging for a Precise person to give up a strategy or procedure that they have a lot of success at following. Two Urgent people can both want to move quickly on different options. Two Reserved individuals may both choose not to talk when talking would be the best solution. Don't assume that similarity on a certain style will be more predictive of communication problems. Issues can crop up in any pairing.

Flexing Guidelines

The following pages provide guidelines for flexing. These are organized under "flexing with opposites" and "flexing with similar individuals." First, select one trait to flex to communicate better with a certain person. Locate that particular match in the lists. Review the guidelines, and then check or mark the suggestions that are most helpful to you when in that particular situation.

Finally, practice implementing the guidelines. This will help you change the interaction pattern between you and the other person. Don't expect the other person to notice and change immediately. It often takes time. This is where patience and persistence pay off.

How ready to change are you?

You may also find it helpful to review the guidelines you checked with the individuals who you are flexing to communicate better with. When they hear what you've identified as efforts you plan to make, they can share their thoughts about which behaviors would be the most helpful. This is invaluable feedback.

Watch for the "teachable moment." Sometimes a wonderful thing happens; they may also ask you what guidelines you would like for them to practice. Stay alert for this opportunity to improve your relationship.

Flexing to Communicate Better with Opposites

Different personalities walk, talk, and phrase things differently. Misunderstandings and conflict may occur not necessarily over what is said, but how it is said. The secret to avoiding communication problems with people who have personality traits opposite from yours is to flex your style so that you communicate in the manner they are most responsive to.

Go into the flexing process with a positive attitude. Every trait has strengths. It is important to value these in yourself and others. This does not mean your strengths and another person's won't create tension or misunderstandings. Anticipate this might happen and plan ahead how to flex your style to minimize problems and actually complement each other.

The following pages present flexing challenges for the opposite preferences of each trait. For example, if you are Indirect you'll focus on the left-hand guidelines that tell how to flex to communicate better with a Direct person. If you're Direct, you'll focus on the guidelines on the right-hand side that help you communicate better with an Indirect person.

You may find it helpful to check specific guidelines that are particularly helpful. If you can identify one or two behaviors to focus on you'll have taken a big step in the right direction. Plan to underline key points, check the most appropriate guidelines, and turn these pages into personalized worksheets.

Attitude check time

The temptation is to wish that others would flex their traits and make it possible for you not to have to flex yours. You may catch yourself thinking, "Why is it that I'm the only one flexing around here?" Sound familiar?

If you do spot yourself thinking this way, then try shifting your thoughts to a more positive attitude that emphasizes your own power and control and your ability as a leader. Say instead things like:

"Wow, isn't is great that I spotted this personality trait difference and have a strategy for working around it!" or "This is an easy adjustment to make. All I have to do is flex a bit here, adjust some there, and communication instantly improves."

Don't expect immediate change in the other person

Even after you make the effort to flex your style, you must not expect that the other person will trust it or make a change. In fact, they will probably think it's an aberration or even an accident on your part. If this is the case, they may ignore you and even double down on their old communication pattern or behavioral preference.

For example, Torin is very Indirect and his father, Oscar, is very Direct. Torin realized that he needed to speak up more when working with his father and not back away from his position on new marketing ideas. In fact, his father often told Torin to stand his ground and not back down if he really believed in his ideas. So, one day Torin did just that. He presented a new idea and was steadfast in defending its merits. But, instead of seeing Torin as flexing and doing exactly what he recommended doing, Oscar got caught up in the problems with the idea and became argumentative, loud, and rather abrasive. Torin left the meeting wondering if flexing had been worth the effort.

Chances are that Torin will have to stand up to his father numerous times before his father will notice it and eventually change his own behavior. The biggest mistake that Torin could make at this time is to give up. He has to accept that just because he flexed his style, it doesn't mean that his Father would immediately notice and change his behavior. But, overtime Torin will alter the dynamic and relationship between them.

To "not give up too soon," is the biggest challenge when learning how to flex your personality traits. If you're lucky, the other person may recognize your efforts and thank you for the adaptations you are making. More than likely, it will take a while. That doesn't mean it's not working. Be prepared to spot small communication changes at first. That is a component of leading with insight.

Instructions

Read the guidelines for each opposite preference on the following facing pages. Check the guidelines that you want to get better at practicing. Then, take some time and identify any additional behaviors you could flex on that trait. Your list will be more personal and memorable to you. You might even identify a person in your life that the flexing behavior would be particularly important to demonstrate.

For example, you might want to list:

I need to be more candid and assertive with Dave, my team leader.
or,
Absolutely be on time and prepared before going into any meeting with Anna.
or,
Make quicker decisions when shopping with my wife or she'll get frustrated.
or
Set my Urgent style aside and be patient with my Steady teenage daughter, Kale, especially when she is around her friends.

Use these activity pages as a way to create a guidebook for communicating with important people in your life.

Go into this activity with a positive attitude. This means that you'll take responsibility to flex first and change your behavior and not wait for them to change first. Remember, flexing is leading; flexing is being a supportive team member; flexing is providing an example; flexing is good parenting; and flexing is giving.

INDIRECT with DIRECT

Guidelines for Indirect people to communicate better with Directs.

There may be times that Direct people see your diplomatic and tactful strengths as softness or even weakness. They may label your Indirect style as wishy-washy, lacking confidence, and being unwilling to take a stand. In some cases, they might accuse you of being secretive.

To flex temporarily to a more Direct style you'll need to:
- Present your ideas and opinions more assertively and forcefully. Direct individuals respect conviction and confidence.
- Stand your ground and be prepared to debate your position. Direct people like to challenge and confront differences.
- Avoid hesitant eye contact, tentative body language, or speaking too softly. Directs may read this as insecurity.

Bottom line, you may need to be more assertive when communicating with Direct individuals. This involves body language and words. Changing your behavior will keep you focused on identifying helpful flexing strategies, rather than thinking that the Direct person is wrong. Drop negative judgments, such as "He's arrogant and stubborn;" "She's overly controlling," "He is bossy." etc. When you go negative, you lose your ability to shift to constructive responses.

List other behaviors that are helpful for an Indirect person to practice when communicating with a Direct individual.

_____

_____

DIRECT with INDIRECT

Guidelines for Direct people to communicate better with Indirect individuals.

Be aware that many Indirect people may not see your confident, assertive behavior as strengths. They may see you as demanding, bossy, and at times as an overwhelming force to deal with.

To communicate better with Indirect individuals:
- Listen thoroughly to Indirect people before debating or arguing your point of view.
- Avoid coming on too forcefully. Indirect people may perceive this as pressure and find ways to escape the discussion or end the meeting.
- Try not to come across too self-assured and overly confident; this may be perceived as arrogance or an air of superiority.
- Watch your body language; don't overpower people with intense eye contact or loud voice volume.
- Find ways to suggest and recommend rather than telling.
- Validate their ideas first, before challenging them.

These guidelines call for you to soften your style and make your comments less emphatic and forceful. This helps assure Indirect individuals that you are open to their input. Using more diplomatic and tactful language lets them know you're seeking a discussion rather than just strongly presenting your foregone conclusions.

List other behaviors you believe are helpful for a Direct person to practice when communicating with an Indirect individual.

_____

_____

RESERVED with OUTGOING

Guidelines for Reserved people to communicate better with Outgoing individuals.

Outgoing individuals may not relate to your self-contained, quiet manner, and may think that you are uninterested in them, shy, or disconnected from your feelings. You'll need to flex your style and generally be more open and expressive.

To communicate better with Outgoing individuals:
- Display more animation and enthusiasm than you normally would. Outgoing people like energy and excitement.
- Spend time getting to know Outgoing individuals personally. Open up and share more about yourself so they don't have to pull information out of you.
- Use expressive mannerisms, smiling, and gestures. Outgoing people trust openness and look for body language to read.

You've probably noticed that all of these guidelines recommend that you move in the direction of being more open and talkative. In terms of body language, this means to smile bigger, laugh louder, touch more frequently, and be as animated as possible.

List other behaviors you believe are helpful for a Reserved person to practice when communicating with an Outgoing individual.

_____

_____

OUTGOING with RESERVED

Guidelines for Outgoing people to communicate better with Reserved individuals.

As an Outgoing individual, you're a people person and you'll seek out connections and relationships with others. You build relationships through open expressions and by freely sharing experiences.

To communicate better with Reserved individuals:

- Listen carefully and don't talk too much or for too long.
- Don't take their quiet style personally.
- Draw Reserved individuals out using open-ended questions and lots of patience. If you ask yes or no questions, you'll get one-word answers.
- Pause after questions before you continue talking, if you don't they will wait you out and avoid answering.
- Don't come across as overly friendly or too touchy-feely, particularly if a relationship isn't established.

Your challenge is becoming a good listener. Since your Reserved friends, co-workers, and family will be rather quiet it is easy to become uncomfortable with this and begin talking yourself again. When its time for you to listen, plan to wait things out and give the Reserved person time to get started talking.

List other behaviors you believe are helpful for an Outgoing person to practice when communicating with a Reserved individual.

_____

_____

URGENT with STEADY

Guidelines for Urgent people to communicate better with Steady individuals.

As an Urgent person, you take action quickly and make decisions fast. However, Steady individuals may see you as restless, impulsive, impatient, and even reckless.

To communicate better with Steady people:
- Hold back some of your snap decisions and take a little more time; Steady people may read your fast decisions as impulsiveness or recklessness.
- Don't pressure Steady individuals into making decisions. Give them plenty of time to think things over.

Try not to react too emotionally to setbacks and delays. Refrain from any critical comments and the tendency to raise your voice, honk your horn, or push the Steady person to speed up. These actions will actually delay them.

Your challenge will be to slow up and be more patient. This will give Steady people time to consider their options and not feel pressured. Even if Steady individuals rush their actions or decisions to please you, they may regret them later and then blame you for forcing them to decide under pressure. It's a no-win situation unless you have an agreement up front when an extra push might be appreciated and they want you to help them by providing that pressure.

List other behaviors an Urgent person could practice when communicating with a Steady individual.

STEADY with URGENT

Guidelines for Steady people to communicate better with Urgent individuals.

Urgent people will frequently appreciate the way you carefully consider options and alternatives before deciding. However, there will be times when they feel you are slowing things down and delaying action. This can be very frustrating to them.

To communicate better with Urgent individuals:
- Present your ideas succinctly. Use quicker speech and snappy gestures. Urgent people like to get to the key points quickly.
- Be ready to change topics and move ahead when Urgent individuals show signs of restlessness or boredom. Don't talk too long on one issue or labor a point.
- Offer to take on aspects of jointly shared projects that make use of your patience, cooperation, and concentration.

Your flexing challenge is to speed things up. Try to find the ideal balance somewhere between your pattern of delaying and thinking things over and the Urgent person's preference for deciding quickly. Be ready to quicken your pace, or at the very least, let Urgent individuals know what you are considering so that they can weigh in with their opinions and feel a sense of involvement.

List other behaviors a Steady person will find it helpful to practice when communicating with an Urgent individual.

_____

_____

UNSTRUCTURED with PRECISE

Guidelines for Unstructured people to communicate better with Precise individuals.

Precise people try to plan their life and work their plan. It's all in the details for them. Since you are Unstructured and flexible, Precise individuals may see you as disorganized and careless with details.

To flex your Unstructured style and communicate more effectively:
- Gather your facts before presenting information and ideas to Precise individuals.
- Be on time and as organized as possible. Precise individuals value timeliness and order.
- Stay on top of details, even when they seem to be trivial.
- Follow work rules and policies, particularly those the Precise individuals believe are important.
- Get your facts and details together before trying to persuade them; use notes and refer to them if necessary.
- Don't let follow-up and details fall between the cracks.

Your flexing challenge is to continue to organize and plan enough that you don't strain your relationships with Precise individuals, yet remain true to your creative ways of doing things. Sometimes you'll need to flex entirely out of your comfort zone and become more organized because some situations and systems require this.

List other behaviors that might be helpful for an Unstructured person to practice when communicating with a Precise individual.

_____

_____

PRECISE with UNSTRUCTURED

Guidelines for Precise people who want to communicate better with Unstructured individuals.

As a Precise person you like to schedule time, organize projects, and attend to details. Unstructured people may see you as overly concerned with minutia, obsessive, and a perfectionist. This means your primary challenge is to loosen up, not be too critical, and yet still maintain the high organizational standards you believe in.

To flex your very Precise style and communicate more effectively with an Unstructured person:

- Stick to the big picture and don't bring up too many small points; Unstructured people often tune out the details.
- Avoid being a perfectionist. Don't try to enforce too many rules. Unstructured people often see this as being nitpicky.
- Hold back your critical remarks regarding what you consider is the other person's lack of organization.
- Don't attempt to get Unstructured individuals to follow all the organizing processes you find helpful.

As a Precise person your challenge is finding that space between your need for order and structure avd being flexible and tolerant. Your mission is to "loosen up without giving up" on your standards, to be more spontaneous and not as critical of others who are unstructured and yet, satisfy your need for some plans, schedules, and systems.

List other behaviors that might be helpful for a Precise person to practice when communicating with an Unstructured individual.

_____

_____

FLEXING with people having SIMILAR traits

People with similar styles usually get along great initially; they act and think alike. Problems arise when they both overuse the same traits and draw out each other's weaknesses rather than building on their shared strengths.

When you first connect and communicate with someone having the same style, you may have noticed:

- from the start you both get along great; you seem to think and behave almost identically.

- the other person communicates in a manner that feels comfortable to you and you are both at ease.

- you are able to establish a good relationship and rapport almost from the beginning.

However, similarity can also bring out patterns of style overuse and weaknesses. What first appeared to be ideal matches can end up strained and fractured. For example, two Indirect individuals may like each other's tactful, diplomatic manner, but since neither candidly says what they are thinking, over time they may get frustrated not knowing where the other person stands on issues.

In a similar fashion, two Direct individuals may initially appreciate each other's forcefulness and candor. But, when tempers flare, they may get into heated arguments because neither is inclined to back down. The advantage of similarity sometimes comes with some disadvantages. That's why it's just as important to also learn how to flex your style when communicating with someone who is like you as it is to flex with people who are different.

The following guidelines will help you identify strategies for flexing your style with people who are similar to you. A good way to begin is to find a specific match that parallels a real-life relationship you have. Then pick just one trait where you are similar and that is causing you some communication problems. Jump forward in the list and locate that specific match, review those guidelines, and pick one or two suggestions you want to practice.

For example, suppose you and the other person are both Urgent and you find yourself going fast in opposite directions on a project. You're both working intensely on two completely different aspects of the project, but the Urgent-x-Urgent guideline recommends that one of you slow down a bit, extend some time on major decisions to avoid overusing your shared urgency.

As you're identifying the areas where you can flex, start by focusing on one or two of the most extreme preferences. That will be challenging enough. You don't have to flex on all the traits at the same time. Usually just one or two traits will be problematic and even then issues may surface only in specific situations or certain types of projects you're both involved in. Scan through the following lists and pick the trait pairings that are most helpful.

Again, use the empty blanks to write some more personalized examples. You can even use the person's name to really help remind yourself who shares a trait with you and how you can flex first to improve communication with that person.

Here are some examples:

Mary and I are both Direct and like to argue. I'll try to listen more and break off discussions if they get too heated rather than fire them up.

Steve and I are two peas in a pod. We're both Reserved and avoid emotional discussions. I'll take a risk and go first next time.

I want to organize the office files a certain way and so does my team member Constance. I'll ask her first how she wants things rather than do it my way without checking.

Scale A: Influencing

INDIRECT and INDIRECT

For two Indirect people to better communicate

Your shared diplomacy will help you communicate well, except when conflict could potentially arise. You'll run into trouble when you have strong differences in your opinions and neither of you is willing to speak up, express those differences, and assert yourself.

To communicate better with another Indirect:

- Use your shared tactfulness to find points of agreement, but take a firm stand on issues important to you.
- Don't avoid conflict when important things need to be discussed and dealt with.
- Encourage each other to be more candid and straightforward when giving each other feedback.

Activity:

List other behaviors you believe an Indirect person could practice when communicating with another Indirect person.

Scale A: Influencing

DIRECT and DIRECT

For two Direct people to better communicate:

Your shared preference for candor and frankness will help you communicate well, except when you have strong differences in your opinions and neither of you wants to give in or compromise your position.

To communicate better with another Direct person:
- Use your shared candor to get right to the point, but be ready to negotiate whose agenda gets addressed first.
- Share control of conversations. You both like to be in charge, so find ways to trade off who has the floor.
- Avoid getting into heated debates. Since you're both Direct, these can turn into confrontations.

Activity:

List other behaviors a Direct person could practice when communicating with another Direct person.

_____

_____

_____

Scale B: Responding

RESERVED and RESERVED

For two Reserved people to better communicate

You'll both tend to be rather quiet, reluctant to initiate emotional conversations, and unlikely to talk much, particularly when in groups.

When communicating with another Reserved individual:

- Take the initiative by speaking first, introducing yourself, and greeting the other Reserved person; don't wait too long or both of you may become uncomfortable.
- Let the person know if anything is on your mind, otherwise important issues may not be discussed.
- Draw out the other person's needs and concerns by asking more personal questions than you might normally do.

Activity:

List other behaviors you believe it would be helpful to practice when communicating with another Reserved person.

_____

_____

_____

Scale B: Responding

OUTGOING and OUTGOING

For two Outgoing people to better communicate

You'll both probably find it easy to strike up conversations and will enjoy each other's enthusiasm, energy, and sense of humor. However, there may be occasions where your similarity and desire to talk causes some tension.

When you're with another Outgoing person:
- Remind yourself to listen more and talk less; otherwise, unnecessary competition for attention may occur.
- Focus conversations on important issues so you don't find yourselves talking about everything but the agenda.
- Avoid creating an imbalance between who is the center of attention. Arrange it so the other Outgoing person can be noticed and heard as much as you.

Activity:

List other behaviors that could be helpful for an Outgoing individual to practice when communicating with another Outgoing person.

_____

_____

_____

Scale C: Pacing

URGENT and URGENT

For two Urgent people to better communicate

You and another Urgent person will both see yourselves as fast-paced and quick to decide. The two of you will work well together on projects and tasks that require quick action. However, there may be situations when your shared urgency leads to impulsive decisions.

To flex your style with another Urgent person:
- Delay decision-making a bit to be sure you and the other person haven't both overlooked some key alternatives.
- Avoid getting tired and impatient and then reactively saying something critical or inflammatory.
- Allow time to double check rushed projects to ensure you both haven't missed critical components.
- Build in time to discuss the direction you have taken on projects before you both go too far down the wrong path.

Activity:

List other behaviors an Urgent person could practice when communicating with another Urgent person.

_____

_____

_____

Scale C Pacing

STEADY and STEADY

For two Steady people to better communicate

You both see yourselves as fairly deliberate, patient, and careful when making decisions. Therefore, there may be situations when your shared steadiness causes the two of you to delay decisions and miss opportunities.

To flex your style to communicate better with a Steady person:
- Speed up the decision-making process so neither of you procrastinates too long.
- Push each other to take action on time-sensitive matters so opportunities aren't overlooked.
- Review and discuss payoffs for deciding quickly so you both feel comfortable making a quick decision.
- Try to help each other identify situations when urgency is a better option than extended patience.

Activity:

List other behaviors you believe are helpful for a Steady person to practice when communicating with another Steady individual.

_____

_____

_____

Scale D: Organizing

UNSTRUCTURED and UNSTRUCTURED

For two Unstructured people to better communicate

Your similarity will help you understand each other's need for flexibility and disinterest in routine details; however, it can also lead to communication problems.

To flex your style to communicate better together:
- Get organized before meeting (because the other Unstructured person probably won't) so you have productive discussions and don't overlook important details.
- Avoid operating too loosely and frustrating each other since neither of you likes dealing with rules and structure.
- Assign each other very specific items to do otherwise you'll both tend to work without structure or order.
- Schedule specific times to attend to details that both of you might normally delay completing

Activity:

List other behaviors an Unstructured person might find it helpful to practice when communicating with other Unstructured people.

_____

_____

_____

Scale D: Organizing

PRECISE and PRECISE

For two Precise people to better communicate

The two of you will tend to be very organized, have a plan and want to put it into action. Your similarity will help you understand and appreciate each other's needs for order, structure, and attention to details; however, it can also lead to communication problems.

To flex your style:
- Restate the plan or big picture once in a while. You'll keep discussions from focusing on details and getting off the larger, more important issues.
- Don't get into debates over whose systems and procedures are the best; both of you can lock in on what you think is the "right" way to do things and may resist changing your methods.
- Carefully phrase your comments about problems you notice or mistakes so you don't seem nitpicky or overly critical.
- Provide each other with lists and procedures to help you be more efficient together; you'll both appreciate this.

Activity:

List other behaviors that are helpful for a Precise person to practice when communicating with another Precise person.

_____

_____

_____

Flexing guidelines work, but not always the first time

The first time or two you flex your style to improve communication, the other person might actually increase the behavior you are hoping to eliminate.

For example, suppose you're an Indirect person and you're with a very Direct person. The first time you flex and come across more assertive, confident, and Direct, the other person might escalate her own Direct assertive behavior because she will be surprised by your energy and her threshold for conflict is high so she'll test you. In this instance, avoid backing down and going back to an Indirect style. You'll need to flex again and again on successive encounters. Eventually you will hit the sweet spot where both of you find that communication flows smoothly.

Flexing gets easier, but it always remains challenging

Over time, the skill at identifying when you need to flex, how you need to flex, and then effectively executing skill at flexing becomes easier. Perhaps the most important part of the process is committing to make flexing a part of your values. The alternative is to take the position that others should flex, not you. As is true with many of the desirable things in life, the process is challenging and at times difficult, but always worth it. The small price to pay for improved communication and enhanced relationships will last forever.

Defining what is fun

Stanley and Mark have been a two-man sales team for many years. Stanley zigs where Mark zags. Stanley is Unstructured and likes to call Mark at the last moment, catch the next flight out of town and go. Mark, on the other hand, is very Precise and structured. He wants things well planned ahead of time. In fact, the trips are much more exciting to him if he knows where he is going and when. He likes to investigate local attractions, museums, and ball games to add some pleasure with business. Sometimes looking forward to the trip and planning it out is as rewarding as the increased business they usually gain.

To lead each other with more insight, Unstructured Stanley learned that the best way to enjoy their time together was to agree to plan a certain number of trips ahead. This was the flexing he had to do. Precise, organized Mark agreed to be open to Stanley's spontaneous sales excursions every so often. This is Mark's flexing and leadership challenge. They both found a way to flex and maintain their long-term and very successful work relationship.

Time to stay home

Karen is very Urgent and when she goes to business conferences to see new products, she is the perfect example of "go, see, buy." Her brand manager, Harold, is Steady and wants to read all the consumer reports, ponder alternatives, and think things over. Harold has learned to flex on this trait. He stays out of the decisions and zips his mouth when the item will primarily impact Karen's department. While he would have taken his time and saved a few dollars he's learned that the disadvantage of creating tension between himself and Karen is not worth the price. Karen leads by flexing her style, and just being patient, very patient when she discusses new products with Harold. She has found that the less she rushes him, the quicker he decides. They've both worked out a way to lead with insight.

Complete the following flexing activity to gain insight into how best to communicate with another person.

FLEXING INSIGHT

AWARENESS

List some traits you have a hard time flexing on at work or at home:

_____

_____

_____

List reasons this trait may change from one environment to another.

_____

_____

_____

UNDERSTANDING

Identify traits you can flex to better your communication with a coworker, friend, or family member.

_____

_____

_____

ACTION

Identify some new actions you can take to flex your style.

_____

_____

_____

When you judge another, you do not define them, you define yourself.
—Wayne Dyer

—//—

Chapter 17

Dropping Judgment

You inherited the ability to make quick judgments from our ancestors. This skill originated from the "drive to survive." Early human hunter-gatherer clans developed the ability to quickly determine whether someone was a friend or a foe. This was a life or death judgment for them. Making the mistake of being too cautious and suspicious was a far safer decision than being too careless and trusting. People could be suspicious and wrong many times, but they could only be trusting and wrong once.

In modern society, the meeting and greeting of strangers is rarely a survival issue. Your success hinges on connecting, relating, and building relationships. Judging others negatively gets in the way of success. Friendships and business relationships form more quickly if you lead with trust and attribute positive characteristics and good intentions to others, rather than negative ones.

Each personality trait assessed by the *INSIGHT Inventory* has positive characteristics. Yet, each of these can be judged as negative when a preference is fairly extreme. An important goal is to learn to see the positive in people's personality traits, particularly when these traits are different from your own.

Suspicion trigger

Jerry, an Indirect Reserved wood working specialist, needed to expand his business. He hired a young apprentice, Ken to help take on some of the extra business. Ken was very Direct and Outgoing. He would strike up conversations with customers and convince them with his self-confidence that he and Jerry could deliver the best product available. However, Jerry had an old negative memory of a previous partner with whom he had a bad business split up. That person was similar to Ken, Outgoing and assertive. Instead of seeing Ken's strengths, Jerry saw every possible negative and became convinced that Ken was out to steal customers, and break away to start a competing business, much as his previous partner had done. This suspicion grew into a trigger and one day, when a minor hot button got pushed, Jerry ended the relationship in an outburst of anger. Ken was stunned and couldn't figure out what had gone wrong.

Behavior is almost always linked to intentionality. Unfortunately, these links are frequently incorrect and represent our negative first, positive second pattern of judging. There is a saying that describes our tendency to mix behavior and intention. "We judge others by their behavior, but we judge ourselves by our intentions." This means we tend to be forgiving and "soft" on ourselves, but judgmental and "hard" on others. Here's how this sometimes plays out.

Misunderstood focus

Jan decides to help Stephen, a new member of her small church, get acquainted. Jan herself is rather Reserved, quiet, and even shy at times. But, she holds an influential position in the church and almost everyone knows her. She thought she could help Stephen and related to the awkwardness he might experience meeting new people. She spotted him in the bookstore and walked in, right past the receptionist, Karen, and warmly grabbed Stephen's arm and asked him to come with her for a tour. She was so intent on helping Stephen that she ignored Karen completely.

Jan's intentions were good if not kind and generous. But, Karen left at the end of the day feeling that Jan was stuck-up and rather cold. Karen judged Jan based on the behavior she witnessed and as it related to her. Karen judged the behavior, not the intention. If Jan had been asked about her day she might have reflected back on her positive intentions of introducing Stephen around. She totally missed noticing that her distracted behavior—walking by Karen without speaking—had been judged by Karen as rudeness and indifference.

Go positive fast, go negative slow

People having opposite personality preferences will tend to judge the other trait negatively at first. This is because they come from such different perspectives. Even when they admire the opposite characteristics, they will frequently see the negative at first. To avoid this, break the old judging pattern by training your brain to think positively and drop its tendencies toward negative judgment. Since negativity is a natural, ancient, historically shaped pattern for humans, it's important to consciously develop more positive attributions and a pattern breaking game plan.

One way to do this is to say to yourself, "go positive fast and go negative slow." Instead of making someone prove that they are deserving of positive attributes, start by "quickly" seeing the best in them and be "slow" in seeing any negatives. To better accomplish this, learn how each of the traits are frequently judged negatively. These patterns are described in upcoming pages. This will help you avoid making these common errors in judgment.

Your childhood influences may also be a factor. If you tend to be negative in your judgments, you may have also learned this tendency from parents, family, classmates, or teachers. Developing a negative pattern is more common unfortunately, than learning a positive orientation. When you develop the unfortunate pattern of seeing the negative first such as being suspicious of other people's intentions, and having your guard up automatically, relationships start with a deficit scorecard. Other people are already problematic in your mind. They can sense this judgment and it forces them to dig out from the negative attributes you've made and prove those were wrong. People instinctively feel this and it can make them defensive. In a way it triggers their trigger of defensiveness.

When negative judgment becomes a pattern, you may believe you're defining others, but you're actually defining yourself. You are setting yourself up to be seen as a critical and distrusting individual. Your ego may want to point out that some people have ill intent and are not to be trusted, and yes, while this is occasionally true, you have to engineer yourself to become the person you want to be. Sometimes this involves growing and developing past some of your old judgments.

Anticipating negative perceptions of your traits.

The following pages provide lists of typical judgments made about each personality trait preference. Read through them and check the ones that have occasionally surfaced in your mind. If you catch yourself practicing any of these, try to find a way to reroute and rewire your thinking. With increased awareness and persistent vigilance, you will be able to override your brain's ancient negative-judging mechanism and grow new neural pathways. These will lead you to more positive, productive relationships. Dropping judgments is one way to transform relationships. When people learn that you are a person who sees the best in them they will change too. A cycle of positive expectations will emerge.

There is also space provided to list any additional judgments you have personally formed or perhaps witnessed people make, about any of the personality traits. Writing these out will help you spot and eliminate them from your own thinking.

Scale A: Influencing
(Indirect and Direct)

When in a negative mindset—

Indirect individuals will tend to judge Direct individuals as:
- arrogant rather than self-confident
- domineering rather than willing to take charge
- abrasive rather than straightforward

List other negative attributions you have witnessed?

- _____

- _____

- _____

Direct people will tend to judge Indirect individuals as:
- weak rather than cautious
- people-pleasing rather than diplomatic
- dishonest rather than tactful

List other negative attributions you have witnessed:

- _____

- _____

- _____

Scale B: Responding

(Reserved and Outgoing)

When in a negative mindset—

Reserved people may judge Outgoing individuals as:
- superficial rather than interested in lots of people
- overbearing rather than talkative
- insincere rather than animated and expressive

List other negative attributions you have witnessed:

- _____

- _____

- _____

Outgoing people may judge Reserved individuals as:
- shy rather than quiet
- uninterested and indifferent rather than self-contained
- aloof rather than just someone who likes time alone

List other negative attributions you have witnessed:

- _____

- _____

- _____

Scale C: Pacing

(Urgent and Steady)

When in a negative mindset—

Urgent people may judge Steady individuals as:

- slow rather than deliberate
- indecisive rather than open to considering options
- tuned out rather than easygoing

List other negative attributions you have witnessed:

- _____

- _____

- _____

Steady people may judge Urgent individuals as:

- impulsive rather than decisive
- reckless rather than opportunistic
- anxious rather than energetic

List other negative attributions you have witnessed:

- _____

- _____

- _____

Scale D: Organizing

(Unstructured and Precise)

When in a negative mindset—

Unstructured people may judge Precise individuals as:
- compulsive rather than highly structured
- perfectionistic rather than having high standards
- rigid rather than planned and scheduled

List other negative attributions you have witnessed:

- _____

- _____

- _____

Precise people may judge Unstructured individuals as:
- unorganized rather than flexible
- messy rather than not requiring order
- lost rather than unscheduled

List other negative attributions you have witnessed:

- _____

- _____

- _____

Attain an Attitude of Altitude

A way to avoid becoming judgmental about certain personality traits is to get some distance. You can do this by removing yourself mentally from the situation. To switch your attitude about something off, pretend you are floating thousands of feet above and just viewing the situation from a distance. This is called "attaining an attitude of altitude." It will help you see emotionally loaded situations more objectively and allow you to drop some of the judgments that arise from being close up and caught up in your immediate reactions.

When someone with a different personality behaves differently than you feel they should, you can also watch this play out from afar. You might rub your chin and say, "Hmmm, how interesting." "Wow, there's an Indirect person who is attempting to get her ideas heard by a very Direct individual and she just can't get his attention because of the way she is wording things." Then, you can think something like, "If I was her I would boldly state three important benefits to the Direct person." That would get his attention.

Gaining this perspective—a view from a distance—helps you move from judgment to non-judgment. An attitude of altitude allows you to more easily see people's strengths and not their weaknesses.

Another familiar and somewhat related phrase is "seeing the forest and not the trees." This also refers to looking at the big picture, the process and the timing of who said what to whom, rather than getting caught up in the content of what was said. This perspective gives you broader insights into situations. It's a process of not getting hooked by people's personalities and triggers. You are accepting who the players are and how they are playing rather than being caught up in the details of the interactions and trying to change them.

Who drops judgment first?

Wouldn't it be nice if others would flex and drop their judgments first and make it possible for you to stay in your comfort zone? Wouldn't it be great if others would do all the work and adapt their style to communicate better with you? Yes, those efforts by others would be nice, but life rarely works out that way. The reality is that if you want the relationships in your life to be positive and the communication to be open, you will need to be the one to take the initiative and flex first to better shape those relationships.

Some people take the position, "I'll change, if you change first!" Or "I'll flex, if you flex first!" Unfortunately, flexing doesn't work that way. If you wait for the other person to flex and change first, you may be waiting for a long time. Plus, you are putting them in control of the relationship. If you become the agent of change and be the one to flex first, you'll have a greater likelihood of improving the dynamics and communication patterns in your relationship.

Wouldn't it be nice?

Wouldn't it be nice if others would see your strengths, perhaps even before you do, and help draw them out? Wouldn't it be nice if others would affirm your personality strengths before they seek to have you see theirs? The reality is that you'll probably need to be the one who sees the other person's strengths first.

The good news is that if you take this initiative and go first, you can shape the tone and character of your relationships. You can shape the relationship as a supportive and positive rather than as negative an judgmental. Actually the goal is to go first and help others see their strengths, grow in positive ways, and realize their potential.

Going first can be difficult in some relationships. If there has been some established patterns of seeing the worst first before you validate the best, you'll have to work on this. It's not for the faint hearted or under committed. When change comes, it will be an immensely rewarding process. When you go first, you take an active role in creating the relationship dynamics you want. As Gandhi is quoted, "be the change you want to see in the world."

Now the challenge

Dropping judgment is a challenging process. Not only is judgment a part of ancient human survival patterns, but many people are raised in rather critical homes and judging others may have become a learned behavioral pattern. When the influences of nature and nurture align, it's unfortunately very easy to become a person who judges negative quickly and sees positive slowly. The good news is that you can change this. Practice awareness, understanding, action.

The first step involves catching yourself and becoming aware of your patterns of judging. The second step involves understanding how you developed this judging behavior and accept that some patterns are natural to humans and some are learned. Still others are reactive and mood based, but they are all manageable. The final step involves taking action, breaking old patterns and rewiring your thinking by seeing strengths rather than weaknesses. This is particularly important for leaders. You want to become a leader who brings out the best in others. That starts by seeing their strengths rather than focusing on their weaknesses.

The phrase, positive judgments, may sound rather awkward at first. It means that when you judge, you try to see the positive intention behind the behavior. Most people are well intended even if their behavior is rather annoying. If you can learn to look past the behavior and focus on what you believe the other person is trying to say, do, or achieve, then you'll become much better at making positive judgments.

Another way of thinking about this is called "Getting yourself out of the issue." When someone complains or makes a critical remark that seems to be judging you, try to focus on what their real goal is. For example, if a co-worker says: "You left the copy machine out of paper." You could take it personal and feel that the other person is judging you as disorganized and inconsiderate. However, if you reword this in your mind and say to yourself that what your co-worker really wants is a way to remind each user to refill the machine when finished. That simple rephrasing drops the judgment and converts the issue into an goal your team will be able to solve. It might become, "How can we set up reminders to refill the copy-machine when it gets low." A simple rethinking of the real intention helps personality differences drop aside and become non-issues.

Creating the habit of seeing positive attributes in yourself and others helps make you a better you. When seeing strengths becomes your natural leadership style, relationships improve, success escalates, and you progress further down the road to becoming the leader you want to be.

As mentioned previously, this takes work. Sometimes hard work. But practice is the solution. The following pages provide a worksheet that will help you learn to drop negative judgments, particularly around personality traits, and shift to a perspective of seeing strengths. Several copies are provided but you may want to make some copies. Breaking patterns takes time. Go easy on yourself. The first few times you try, you may only get to Step 1. That's still an improvement over being unaware. Try to make it a practice to catch at least one judgment a day for a couple of weeks and see how much more aware you become of judgments you make, how much better you understand where these old patterns are coming from, and how much easier it becomes to take new actions. You'll find yourself automatically leading better as you incorporate this Awareness—Understanding—Action model into your leadership behavior.

DROPPING JUDGMENT WORKSHEET

A key to unleashing your personality strengths involves learning to drop your judgment patterns and see the strengths of others.

Step 1: AWARENESS

List a judgment about personality traits that you made today:

_____

_____

Step 2: UNDERSTANDING

List a possible reason or memory that may explain how you formed this judgment. (childhood experiences, comments from parents, teachers, and friends, or old family patterns, etc.)

_____

_____

Step 3: ACTION

Refer to your personality strengths and list a replacement behavior that you would rather use in the future.

_____

_____

DROPPING JUDGMENT WORKSHEET

A key to unleashing your personality strengths involves learning to drop your judgment patterns and see the strengths of others.

Step 1: AWARENESS

List a judgment about personality traits that you made today:

_____

_____

Step 2: UNDERSTANDING

List a possible reason or memory that may explain how you formed this judgment. (childhood experiences, comments from parents, teachers, and friends, or old family patterns, etc.)

_____

_____

Step 3: ACTION

Refer to your personality strengths and list a replacement behavior that you would rather use in the future.

_____

_____

DROPPING JUDGMENT WORKSHEET

A key to unleashing your personality strengths involves learning to drop your judgment patterns and see the strengths of others.

Step 1: AWARENESS

List a judgment about personality traits that you made today:

_____

_____

Step 2: UNDERSTANDING

List a possible reason or memory that may explain how you formed this judgment. (childhood experiences, comments from parents, teachers, and friends, or old family patterns, etc.)

_____

_____

Step 3: ACTION

Refer to your personality strengths and list a replacement behavior that you would rather use in the future.

_____

_____

There are three things extremely hard: steel, a diamond, and to know one's self.
—Benjamin Franklin

One's own self is well hidden from one's own self;
of all mines of treasure, one's own is the last to be dug up.
—Friedrich Wilhelm Nietzsche

—//—

Chapter 18

Unleashing Strengths

As a quick review; so far, you've:

- identified a vision for becoming who you want to be

- learned the positive characteristics of your personality traits

- examined your profile shape and interactions between traits

- explored how you may change from setting to setting

- looked at how you can overuse a strength when under stress

- spotted triggers and hot buttons that throw you out of your strengths

- identified strategies for flexing to communicate better with others

- explored how to drop negative judgment patterns

Next you'll focus on unleashing your unique strengths. Your special leadership style will unfold from your strengths. There have probably been times in your past when you did just that and maybe didn't quite realize it. Sometimes personality strengths are revealed by life's challenges. At other times, they emerge when special opportunities present themselves.

Think back to a time you rose to the occasion as a leader when a crisis surfaced and there was an urgent problem to solve. Perhaps you had a lucky break and you seized an opportunity. Maybe a special person, parent, teacher, or coach saw something unique in you and helped you see this quality also. An activity at the end of this chapter will help you go further in identifying some of your personality strengths and exploring how they emerged. Think of some examples from your past, that reflect how you discovered, rediscovered, or unleashed one of your personality strengths as a leader.

It is never too late to discover your "true" you. Not long ago a simple note arrived in the mail. It said "Thank you." That short appreciation would have been sufficient, and much appreciated, yet the author, who was anticipating her 70th birthday, went on to say that a recent *INSIGHT Inventory* seminar had helped her discover and unleash a side of her that she had suppressed for over 65 years. She revealed that it was a personality trait she had as a child, but then hid away to try to be who others had wanted her to be. She was thankful for having a pathway to rediscover it and unleash it.

She didn't say, that it was too late to change. She didn't complain about the reason for hiding that particular strength. Nor, did she list a set of regrets. Instead, she enthusiastically looked forward to being all she could be for the rest of her life. Her attitude was inspiring. It is never too late to unleash your unique personality strengths.

As a leader, unleashing your strengths is all about becoming the "true" you and then practicing sound leadership practices.. Just like the image of the fingerprint on the front cover of this book, you have many colors and hues. Your special set of personality strengths is unique.

Since everyone sees color through their own shaded lenses, others may see you differently. That's okay. If you can help them share their observations of your behavior as a leader (a sign of trust), you can use what you learn to improve communication.

We all start out on this journey in life with so much potential and a set of personality strengths that are waiting to emerge. However, as a small child you were immediately faced with a force field around you. Some behaviors were encouraged, others were tolerated, and still others were discouraged. If you've ever wondered how your personality might have developed if you were raised in a different setting, a different family, a different country, or perhaps even a different time and age, then you're pondering how the environment might have impacted you.

Most of the influences from family and educators were probably well intentioned. This doesn't mean they were "right" for you, a bit too extreme, or even dysfunctional. For whatever reason, some of your personality strengths might have been stressful to your parents or family members. You might have triggered their triggers. They may have been repeating some of the old child-rearing patterns that their parents used with them. Some patterns, good or bad, may have been passed on to you by your parents. They in turn may have learned these patterns from earlier generations. Rescanning your past to uncover old learned triggers gives you a solid base to continue your self-discovery.

Safety over adventure

Kevin is thriving under the leadership of Kelly. She encourages him to take risks and try new marketing approaches. He enjoys this new-found freedom. However, not long before transferring to Kelly's department he almost quit the company. When Kevin worked under a different supervisor who worried about every possible outcome this leadership style paralyzed Kevin.

He realized other people's fearful reactions to risk was a trigger for him. As a child he recalls being a self-confident, urgent, and fast-acting. When he got something in his head that he wanted to do he was strong-willed and spontaneous. This was rather frightening to his single mother who wanted to keep him under control and safe. She was an indirect, cautious, steady individual and not a risk taker. When Kevin was a child she issued many precautions such as, "slow down," "don't run," and "be careful." Then, as a young teenager, he was discouraged from getting involved in risky sports such as mountain climbing, horseback riding, etc. To please his mother, he learned to be cautious and hesitant.

Now in his career, and away from a supervisor who in a way, reminded him of his mother, he is succeeding beyond expectations. Kelly, as a leader who somehow sensed that Kevin needed his freedom and support, has brought out an innate personality trait of his that sat dormant because of old learned behaviors.

In every setting or environment, some behaviors are encouraged and some are discouraged. A leader can unconsciously restrict the emergence personality strengths in employees. Reflecting back, you may recall that you yourself may have buried some strengths while working for a particular leader. While that was unfortunate, you can use that to propel you to become just the opposite type of leader. You can become a leader who brings out people's strengths.

Finding oneself

Willis was born into a family of extroverted, Direct, strong minded individuals. He never seemed to be able find his voice or to engage in the loud laughter and sarcastic humor which the other family members enjoyed so much. It wasn't until he left home that he discovered that instead of being shy and retiring, he was somewhat Direct and Outgoing. He found in many situations he actually had a strong voice and a warm engaging manner.

Willis's parents' extreme styles had been so distorted in his eyes as a child that he didn't grow up with a perspective of what was normal. As he unleashed his assertiveness and grew in responsiveness, he eventually embarked on a career in state politics and was very popular. Reflecting back on his childhood, Willis realized that he had given up his voice because he always felt out-debated and overpowered by his more extreme assertive and dramatic parents. Willis had pulled into a shell and remained there until years later when, as a popular political leader, he learned to unleash his strengths.

Getting it together

Lori, a very Steady and Precise child, grew up in a very unstructured and unpredictable environment. Her family was in the entertainment business and continually moved from place to place touring with country western bands, horse shows, and the rodeos. Her brothers and sisters were in the show with their parents and never seemed to mind the makeshift life they led from sleeping in motels, living in temporary apartments, and homeschooling with various tutors. Lori's brothers saw it as a magical, "free" life compared to the boring humdrum existence their friends described in typical suburban homes.

However, Lori was often anxious and a doctor prescribed sedatives and sleeping pills in her teenage years to help her relax. Even then, she just couldn't seem to adapt. After leaving home, she joined the military service and found a place in the quartermaster inventory control network. Her primary responsibility was tracking the details of supplies and logistics of a small base in an isolated location. Life was predictable. She thrived because she could make good use of her need for structure and attention to detail. She became a leader and as the officer in charge, she relaxed, stopped worrying, and poured her energy into maintaining consistency and predictability. She became exactly what that military base needed as a leader and was promoted again and again. She unleashed her personality strengths, comfortably settled into a career lifestyle that she absolutely loved.

In Lori's case, her Steady and Precise nature had caused her to feel uncomfortable and stressed in her childhood. She could not unleash the innate personality strength of those traits until she found the right setting where they were needed and appreciated. In Willis's case, he felt restrained in childhood and didn't discover his more outgoing leadership style until later. These examples clarify why it is so important to continually think about who you really are and could be as a leader if you unleash your personality strengths.

So, how do you do this? To get started leading with insight, become a learn-a-holic about the one and only "you." Some people quit learning about themselves after they reach adulthood. They say, "This is who I am." Or, they claim, "I've always been this way and probably won't change." Those comments will restrict you. There are always more strengths that you can identify and unleash in new and different ways. There will always be situations that will bring out your best and situations that will hold you back. Find more of the first. There are also many trait triggers you may trip over that will bind up and hide your strengths. Strive to eliminate them.

Fortunately, there are always ways for you to flex and improve relationships, communication, and your leadership skills. It's important to value who you are, and who you have become, but do not let your self-development rest. Continually look for ways to get better. Make the revealing of your true, unique you, an enjoyable, inspiring, lifelong process.

An interesting thing may happen when you lead with insight and become your "true" you. Others around you may begin doing the same. It becomes contagious in a beautiful way. Your new freedom, to lead both yourself and others with insight, evokes something in others. As you start to see them differently their personality strengths will unfold in your presence. Maybe increased control over your hot buttons stops triggering others and straining relationships and those relationships improve. Each of these possibilities begins after you take the first step and you decide to *LEAD with INSIGHT.*

Perhaps a good place to end this book is with the beginning. Reread the opening poem. Then take a moment and identify some personality strengths you want to practice more often in your journey in becoming the leader who you want to be.

> *The three of you go down the road,*
> *as down the road go you,*
> *the one you know,*
> *the one they see,*
> *and the one you want to be.*

Personality strengths you want to lead with as you go down the road:

_____

_____

_____

_____

Enjoy the journey!

——Patrick Handley

APPENDIX

Statistics and Norming of INSIGHT Inventory

This section provides a summary of theoretical development, research design, norming, reliability, and validity. A detailed manual with comprehensive tables and validation date is available at: *INSIGHT Inventory*, Facilitator Success Center web page— www.insightinventory.com/successcenter/index.html

Technical Manual Snapshot

Research and Theoretical Background

The *INSIGHT Inventory* has been thoroughly researched and developed by Patrick Handley, Ph.D. a licensed psychologist. To insure unbiased data analysis, consultation was provided by Dr. Thomas Krieshock. He was past Chairman and current faculty member at the Department of Education and Counseling Psychology, at the University of Kansas.

Independent review

The *INSIGHT Inventory* has received favorable reviews (plus constructive feedback) by the independent test review authority, the Buro's Mental Measurement Yearbook. Numerous doctoral and master's theses have been completed on the *INSIGHT Inventory*. The data is publically available in the Insight Technical Manual.

Reliability
Test-retest and inter-item reliability coefficients were within the acceptable ranges (.70 to .75) of recommended levels.

Validity

The validity of the scales was established using comparisons to several other respected assessments: The 16PF, MBTI, Holland Code, Big 5, and correlational data provides strong support of trait names and construct validity.

Norming

Normative data is provided and also periodically updated. The information in this has been abbreviated and condensed. The complete Technical Manual is available at:www.insightinventory.com/facilitator

If you don't have time to do it right, when will you have time to do it over?
—John Wooden

—//—

Reliability, Validity, and Norming

Understanding the background theory and statistical research of the *INSIGHT Inventory* can be helpful in interpreting and understanding your results. This chapter provides a brief overview.

Since technical manuals can be rather intimidating, the following overview is written in non-technical terms and conversational language. The results are presented in broad stroke references with short descriptions of the meaning and usage of the statistical terms. Please reference the Technical Manual for specifics and details that go beyond the scope of this book.

Original vision

The *INSIGHT Inventory* was developed to provide a strengths-based report that describes personality traits in an easy-to-use, conservational language. The primary objective in the design of the *INSIGHT Inventory* was to identify personality traits that are commonly expressed in daily interactions between people at work and in their personal life. The assessment recognizes that behavior is not the same in all environments; therefore, it helps you identify how you may change your behavior from one setting to another.

The *INSIGHT Inventory* is not intended to be a comprehensive assessment of all possible personality traits. Instead it is a measure of four of the traits most commonly used when people communicate in groups, whether the group is a work team, gathering of friends, or family unit.

The *INSIGHT Inventory* originates as much from the field of social psychology and anthropology as it does from the area of psychology and psychometrics. Since it measures traits that people display in group interactions and daily behavior it may peak your interest in how and why certain personality traits developed in humans. Another related field, social anthropology, studies how the psychology of the individual emerges through the shaping of humans in early tribal clans up to modern social groups. This also greatly influenced the development of the *INSIGHT Inventory*. Its clear that certain personality traits surfaced to best serve people in groups. Plus, it must have been beneficial to have a wide range of differences in the distribution of these traits. Therefore, many traits developed.

Humans are group oriented. People like to be in groups. Whether the group is a tribe, clan, family, or mega society, it's important for us to fit in and be accepted. Therefore, we evolved personality traits to help accomplish this. Once human beings form into their primary groups, they have a need to establish their position. We still replicate this. Since groups get complex quickly, particularly as the size of the group increases, there is a need for a wide range of assertiveness in the group. Some individuals will need to be more dominate and seek to take charge. Others will need to be more cooperative and be willing to follow, at least for a while until they get their chance to be in charge.

Then, we have this core need to create and contribute. Perhaps it had something to do with being valued and accepted, probably a good reason to be retained in the group in ancient times. This may have led to our current level need to contribute and have a purpose in life; also a good thing. But eons ago this may have more likely helped us develop different ways of doing things and various degrees of urgency and patience.

These original thoughts and inclinations for assessment scales were all interesting, but to follow a scientific approach these theories had to be put aside. A broad range of test items were selected and a proven statistical process, factor analysis, was used to identify what the items were actually measuring.

The desire was to build a "better mousetrap" and use scientific, research-based processes to do this. Other objectives were to make it positive and strengths based, take into account how people can change their behavior from one setting to another, not lock anyone into a box or label them in a limiting way, and use everyday, conversational language so the results were easy to discuss with co-workers, family members, and friends.

Development

The *INSIGHT Inventory* owes its theoretical heritage to three primary sources: the work done by Kurt Lewin on field theory, Gordon Allport's use of adjectives in the measure of personality traits and his writings on insight as the cornerstone of mature personality, and Raymond Cattell's application of factor analysis for identifying personality traits and determining the relatedness of test items.

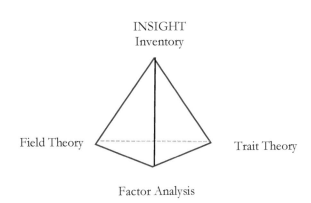

Field Theory

Field Theory, developed and popularized by Dr. Kurt Lewin (1890-1947) emphasized that behavior (B) can best be understood in the context of the personality of the individual (P) and the environment the behavior occurs within (E). This was represented in the formula, $B = f(P \times E)$. The *INSIGHT Inventory* asks participants to describe how they behave in two important environments, their world at work (or school) and their personal world. The two profiles produced help people explore how these two different environments impact their behavior and help them better understand why they behave the way they do.

Trait Theory

The use of adjectives as test items for the measure of personality traits was first formally studied and given scientific credence by Dr. Gordon Allport (1897-1967). Allport and Odbert (1936) identified over 4500 words in the English language that they felt described personality characteristics. These were divided into what was believed to represent various types of traits, dispositions, habits, attitudes, intentions, and motives. As a trait theorist, Allport wrote extensively about *insight* which he felt represented the mature personality, one characterized by self-awareness, acceptance, and good humor. The *INSIGHT Inventory* credits its name to Allport's emphasis on insight, which he called the most desirable of all traits.

Factor Analysis

Dr. Raymond Cattell (1905-1998) pioneered the technique of using factor analysis to identify the most powerful factors of a personality test. Items (adjectives) on the *INSIGHT Inventory* were selected based on statistical analysis of their factor loadings. This resulted in the creation of personality scales that give people a meaningful and scientific way to compare themselves to others.

Statistics, Reliability, & Validity

To insure unbiased reporting, an independent review and data analysis were conducted at the Department of Counseling Psychology, at the University of Kansas. In addition, the *INSIGHT Inventory* has received favorable reviews by the independent test review authority, the *Buro's Mental Measurement Yearbook*. Plus, numerous doctoral and master's theses have been completed on the *INSIGHT Inventory*.

Reliability

Reliability is the degree of consistency with which a test measures what it is said to measure. Test length greatly affects reliability coefficients, with longer tests traditionally producing higher scores. Dr. J.C. Nunnally stated in the classic reference book, Psychometric Theory, © 1978, that internal consistency reliability coefficients for short personality tests should range in the .70's to .80's. For example, the well-researched Myers-Briggs Type Indicator reports internal consistency reliability for its four scales on general population samples to range from .61 to .87. Internal consistency reliability was computed on each of the four scales of the much shorter *INSIGHT Inventory* and the results ranged from .71 to .85. Thirty-day test-retest reliability produced scores ranging from .76 to .82. Given its very short length, the *INSIGHT Inventory* produced very solid reliability coefficients.

Validity

The validity scores of a test estimate how well the test measures what it claims to measure. Personality assessment tests usually produce validity scores for each of the individual traits measured. When scores on the traits of a test correlate well with scores on similar traits on other tests, the test is said to have good concurrent validity.

Validity coefficients were computed on each of the four *INSIGHT Inventory* traits by comparing these to the traits measured by the Myers-Briggs Type Indicator (MBTI), Sixteen Personality factors (16PF), and Holland Self-Directed Search (SDS). Very strong support for the validity of the traits measured by the *INSIGHT*

Inventory was garnered. This data comprises a large section of the INSIGHT Technical Manual and users are encouraged to review those pages and tables.

Technical Characteristics

The *INSIGHT Inventory* is a self-report, personality inventory that measures the intensity of four bipolar traits: Scale A–Influencing, Direct or Indirect; Scale B–Responding, Reserved or Outgoing; Scale C–Pacing, Urgent or Steady; and Scale D–Organizing, Unstructured or Precise. Thirty-two terms, primarily adjectives and short descriptive phrases derived through factor analysis, make up the item pool. Based on Kurt Lewin's Field Theory, the *INSIGHT Inventory* measures behavior in two environments (fields). Participants first rate how they see themselves at work (field 1). Then, they rate how they see themselves at home (field 2). The *INSIGHT Inventory* takes approximately ten minutes to complete.

Item Analysis

Item analysis establishes the statistical relationship between items of an inventory and the traits they measure. If no item analysis is done then the matching of an item to a particular trait is essentially a guess on the test developer's part. An initial sample of 1540 individuals completed the *INSIGHT Inventory* and a factor analysis of their scores was computed to select the items that loaded most heavily on the four factors (scales).

The validity correlations, the relationship of the four factors to other assessments, were then reviewed and the names of the scales were selected. The overriding goal was to name the traits using conversational language and to use terminology that was as neutral as possible. This helps insure that people feel that is okay to score anywhere on any trait and be open to discussing their results with others. In the end, that is what is most important. If people can feel good about their results, then they can be open to sharing them and talking with others about their similarities and differences. This is when the real magic happens, people discover ways to communicate better with each other, how not to take others personally, and how to see the strengths in everyone.

The comprehensive technical manual can be accessed at the Success Center at: www.insightinventory.com/facilitator.

If you have an interest in using the *INSIGHT Inventory* for further research, please contact us at: customerservice@insightinstitute.com

POEM CREDIT

Sometimes the credit for a great poem is lost in time. So it appears to be with the verse used to guide the structure of this book. Research and web searches produce conflicting results. The following version is credited to John Masefield (1838-1967) as possibly penned sometime in the late 1890's in England. Other sources cite just "Anonymous" and the 1920's.

One version:
Three men went down the road,
as down went he.
The one he was,
the one they saw,
and the one he wanted to be.

a second, slightly different version, also credited to Masefield
And there were three men whom went down the road,
As down the road went he.
The man they saw,
The man he was,
And the man he wanted to be.

In search of the author I shared the poem with colleagues in the United Kingdom. They felt the tone and tenor match *Sea Fever.* Indeed, it flows very similarly in cadence and supports the theory that *Three Men* may be his work.

Sea Fever by John Masefield (first verse)
I must go down to the seas again, to the lonely sea and the sky,
And all I ask is a tall ship and a star to steer her by,
And the wheel's kick and the wind's song and the white sail's shaking,
And a grey mist on the sea's face, and a grey dawn breaking.

REFERENCES

Allport, G.W. (1955), *Theories of Perception and the Concept of Structure.* New York: Wiley.

Allport, G.W. & Odbert, H.S. (1936). *Trait-Names: A Psycho-lexical Study.* Princeton: Psychological Review Company.

Allport, G.W. (1947). *The Genius of Kurt Lewin.* J. Pers., 16, 1-10.

Allport, G.W. (1937). *Personality: A Psychological Interpretation.* New York: Holt.

Allport, G.W. (1950a). *The Nature of Personality:* Selected papers. Cambridge, Mass.: Addison-Wesley.

Allport, G.W. (1955). *Becoming Basic Considerations for a Psychology of Personality.* New Haven: Yale University Press.

Allport, G.W. (1961). *Pattern and Growth in Personality.* New York: Holt, Rinehart and Winston.

Allport, G.W. (1966). *Traits Revisited.* American Psychologist, 21, 1-10.

American Psychological Association (1983). *Publication Manual of the American Psychological Association.* Washington, D.C.: Author.

American Psychological Association (1985). *Standards for Educational and Psychological Testing.* Washington, D.C.: Author.

Anastasia, A. (1976). *Psychological Testing.* New York: MacMillan Publishing Co., Inc.

Cattell, R.B. (1943). *The Description of Personality: Basic Traits resolved into clusters.* The Journal of Abnormal and Social Psychology, 36.

Cattell, R.B. (1946). *Description and Measurement of Personality.* Yonkers-on-Hudson: World Book Co.

Cattell, R.B. (1947). *Confirmation and clarification of primary personality factors.* Psychometrika, 12, 197-220.

Cattell, R.B., Eber, H.W. & Tatsuoka, M. (1980). *Handbook for the Sixteen Personality Factor Questionnaire (16PF).* Champaign: Institute for Personality and Ability Testing.

Cattell, R.B. (Ed.). (1966b). *Handbook of Multivariate Experimental Psychology.* Chicago: Randy McNally.

Cattell, R.B. (1957). *Personality and Motivation Structure and Measurement.* New York: Harcourt, Brace & World.

Gough, H.G. (1965). *The Adjective Check List Manual.* Palo Alto, California: Consulting Psychologists Press.

Handley, P.G. (1982). *The Relationship Between Supervisors' and Trainees' MBTI Styles and the Supervision Process.* Journal of Counseling Psychology, 29, 508-515.

Hartshorne, H., & May, M.A. (1930). *Studies in the nature of character.* III. Studies in the organization of character. New York: MacMillan.

Holland, J.L. (1973). *Making Vocational Choices: A Theory of Careers.* New Jersey: Prentice Hall.

Kaiser, K.M. (1981) *Use of the First 50 Items as a surrogate measure of the Myers-Briggs Type Indicator Form G.* Research on Psychological Type.

Krug, S.E. (1983). *Interpreting 16PF Profile Patterns.* Champaign: Institute for Personality and Ability Testing.

Lewin, K. (1935). *A Dynamic Theory of Personality.* New York: McGraw-Hill, 1935.

Lewin, K. (1936b). *Some Social-Psychological Differences Between the United States and Germany.* Character and Personality, 4, 265-293.

Lewin, K. (1936a). *Principles of Topological Psychology.* New York: McGraw-Hill.

Lewin, K. (1948). *Resolving social conflicts;* Selected papers on group dynamics. Gertrude W. Lewin (Ed.). New York: Harper & Row.

Lewin, K. (1951). *Field theory in social science;* Selected theoretical papers. D. Cartwright (Ed.). New York: Harper & Row.

Lewin, K. (1954). *Behavior and development as function of the total situation.* In L. Carmichael (Ed.). Manual of child psychology. New York, Wiley, 918-970.

MacDaid, G.P. (1983) *A Comparison of Myer-Briggs Form G and Form H.* Paper presented at APT-V, College Park, MD.

Myers, I.B. (1962) *Myers-Briggs Type Indicator Manual.* Palo Alto, California: Consulting Psychologists Press.

Myers, I.B. & McCaulley, M.M. (1985). *Manual: A Guide to the Development and Use of the Myers-Briggs Type Indicator.* Palto Alto: Consulting Psychologists Press.

Nunnally, J.C., (1978). *Psychometric Theory.* New York: McGraw-Hill Book Company.

Sealy, A.P., and Cattell, R.B. Adolescent personality trends in primary factors measured in the 16PF and the HSPQ questionnaires through ages 11-23. *Brit. J. Soc. Clinical Psychology,* 1959, 15, 3-21.

Thurstone, L.L. Multiple factor analysis. *Psychology Review.* 1931, 38, 406-427.

Thurstone, L.L. *Multiple factor analysis: a development and expansion of the vectors of the mind.* Chicago: University of Chicago Press, 1947.

Thurstone, L.L. Psychological implications of factor analysis. American Psychologist, 1948, 3, 402-408.

Tolman, E.C. Kurt Lewin, 1890-1947. Psychological Review, 1948, 55, 1-4.

PATRICK HANDLEY, Ph.D.
Psychologist, Organizational Consultant, Coach, Author

Dr. Patrick Handley is a licensed psychologist, management consultant, author, speaker, and coach. He founded the Insight Institute, Inc., an organization that created and now publishes the *INSIGHT Inventory* and supporting leadership training resources, team development, and personal growth materials.

The *INSIGHT Inventory* is published in adapted versions for businesses, schools, couples, families, and teens. It has been used internationally by corporate trainers, coaches, and educators in to help people increase self-understanding and improve personal effectiveness.

Dr. Handley received his Ph.D. in counseling psychology from the University of Missouri in 1980. His degree emphases were in personality assessment, career development, and organizational development. He has held faculty and counseling center appointments at two universities, Virginia Polytechnic Institute and the University of Missouri. He was employed in business as a leadership development specialist and training director before founding his own company, the Insight Institute, Inc.

Dr. Handley continues to conduct seminars, workshops, and *INSIGHT Inventory* certification sessions. With over three decades of speaking experience, Dr. Handley provides fast-paced entertaining sessions packed with practical how-to information that participants can easily relate to and apply immediately.

Dr. Handley strives to incorporate messages of tolerance and acceptance for not only various personality trait strengths, but for all differences between people, their cultures, and backgrounds. He resides in Kansas City, Missouri, with his wife Melanie and their two college age children. He is also an accomplished oil painter and has a passion for raising and training horses.

Seminars and workshops using the INSIGHT Inventory

Do you want to help associates in your organization,
- improve personal effectiveness?
- unleash their personality strengths?
- increase productivity, teamwork, and performance?

Consider the following training programs and presentations and explore other select presentations at www.drpatrickhandley.com

Improving Personal Effectiveness
Participants identify their personality strengths and learn how to see the best in themselves and others, communicate more effectively, and use their strengths in more productive ways.

Eliminating Triggers, Hot Buttons, and Career Derailers
Participants learn how to eliminate touchy reactions, triggers, and hot buttons that move them away from their personality strengths. The session focuses on increasing emotional fitness and skill at defusing their own triggers and avoiding getting hooked on other people's hot buttons.

Leading People and Developing Team Talent
Participants identify their personality strengths and learn how to use them to increase leadership success. They learn how their traits motivate certain team members but create communication challenges for others. An emphasis is put on learning how to flex leadership behavior based on team stages and the needs of each team member. The focus is on how to be the leader the team needs and how to motivate different people differently.

Develop People, Unleash Potential, Grow Talent

About Insight Institute, Inc.

We develop people.
With our best-known product, the *INSIGHT Inventory*, now celebrating over thirty years of publication we continue to apply positive psychology and strengths-based personality assessment to individual and team development. We focus on 1) bringing out the best in people and 2) helping organizations develop strengths-based teams, 3) enhancing talent potential, and 4) improving organizational cultures.

We unleash potential.
We unleash the potential of individuals by helping them develop skill in communication, team leadership, and team membership. Often, team members are left out of the talent develop equation and organizations instead over teach and over train leaders. This leaves the members of teams underdeveloped and often resisting change. We help team members learn how to maximize the use of their personality strengths and validate the strengths of each other and the team leader. Bottom line, we help teams create high functioning cultures that unleash potential and retain top talent.

We engage talent.
Talent is either engaged and growing or disengaged and degrading. We help talent identify and stay in their strengths zone and eliminate the triggers, hot buttons, and stress reactions that derail success.

www.insightinstitute.com

About INSIGHT Inventory

The INSIGHT Inventory is a positive, strengths-based personality assessment with targeted interpretative booklets and online reports. Insight assessments measure self-perceptions, how others view the users, and plots patterns, gaps, and overlaps on team maps.

Available in both paper self-scoring versions and online digital reports.

Self

Users identify their personality strengths, learn how and why they change from one setting to another, spot stressors, triggers and hot buttons and then identify ways to flex their strengths to communicate better with others. The self-scoring paper booklet is ideal for seminars and workshops.
(This book contains a code for one digital self-report report)

Observer

The *Observer Feedback Reports* help people learn how others see them. They can compare these to their self-report and discover differences in perceptions. These reports (users should get several) are ideal for better understanding differences and resolving conflict.

Team Map

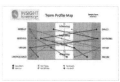

The *Insight Team Map* plots the scores of all members of a group on one colorful chart. Teams can immediately spot gaps and overlaps and identify ways to work better together. Use for team building, communications improvement, and couples coaching.

www.insightinventory.com

Have fun with self-discovery

If you are presenting team building session or conference and you want a way to add some fun and increase conversations about strengths – consider providing everyone a T-shirt.

Option 1: Wear them "as is" as a reminder of the conference or team building session.
or
Option 2: Use them as a powerful discussion activity. Ask participants to write specific, positive descriptive terms on the back of each other's shirt. It's really fun if they are wearing the T-Shirts and have different color markers. The energy goes up. participants can't wait to see what was written on their shirt. Plus, they treasure these for years to come.

Check out sizes and options.

Contact:
customerservice@insightinstitute.com

Complete the online INSIGHT Inventory

To create your account and complete the self-assessment go to:
www.einsightinventory.com

Enter Access Code: **MG7510F21**

FIRST TIME

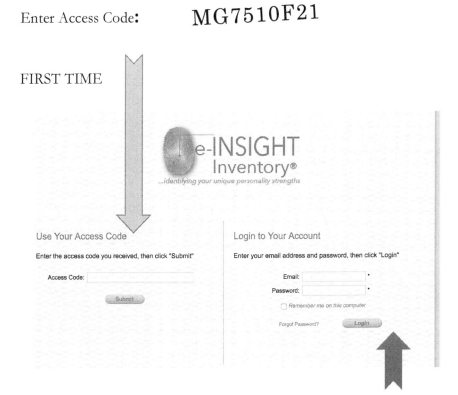

RETURNING

Once you set up your complimentary account you can return any time—using the email and password you created—and view your SELF report and set up Observer Feedback reports.

For assistance contact:
customerservice@insightinstitute.com